THE
PROPHETIC
MADE
PERSONAL

THE PROPHETIC MADE PERSONAL

SECRET KEYS TO UNLOCKING YOUR PERSONAL DESTINY

MICKEY ROBINSON

DESTINY IMAGE® PUBLISHERS, INC.
P.O. Box 310, Shippensburg, PA 17257-0310

"Speaking to the Purposes of God for this Generation and for the Generations to Come."

This book and all other Destiny Image, Revival Press, MercyPlace, Fresh Bread, Destiny Image Fiction, and Treasure House books are available at Christian bookstores and distributors worldwide.

For a U.S. bookstore nearest you, call 1-800-722-6774.
For more information on foreign distributors, call 717-532-3040.
Reach us on the Internet: www.destinyimage.com.

ISBN 10: 0-7684-3152-2
ISBN 13: 978-0-7684-3152-0

For Worldwide Distribution, Printed in the U.S.A.
1 2 3 4 5 6 7 8 9 10 11 / 14 13 12 11 10

Dedication

I dedicate this book to all the beautiful people
Over this world, who have received our humble offering,
Blessed us with kind words of encouragement,
Celebrated with joy my imperfections, while perceiving
God's gifts being delivered for the common good of us all,
For allowing me to grow in a lifelong learning process.

Special honor to my life's partner, Barbara.
You are a true mystic and
You are a revelation, a sign, and a wonder.

To Michael: champions go the distance; finish well.

To all those who are hungry to know Him
and to make Him known.

Acknowledgments

Our son, Matt, and his lovely wife, Natasha—Matt, you have been a comfort to me; may all your dreams come true. Our son, Jacob, and the perfect match, Sommer—what great parents to Elijah and Shiloh you have become. You are both strong yet tender. May the blessings of the Lord overtake you. My little peach Elizabeth—you always bring the fireworks with you! Bryan, you are a special man of grace and wisdom; you and Sis, Ariel, Merci, and the new sweet girl will rock the world. Any prophecy concerning blessings in our lives that Mom and I have received is fulfilled in your lives growing in grace before our eyes. You're the best.

James Goll and family—the last 25 percent of my life in ministry has been deeply involved with you, and what a ride it's been. You have colors that are not even on the visible spectrum. Keep letting your light shine. More people will see you as you really are. I have been privileged to know you in a special way and I will jealously guard that as special treasure from the Lord. Thanks for the anointing, the tears, and the fun!

George Barrett, Bob Kutz (gone to his reward), Roger Pugh, and Jim Stevens—our exploits together have been heroic, hilarious, unprecedented pioneering, and more valuable than we will probably ever know.

To the family at Destiny Image—Don Sr., you were doing it before anybody ever heard of it. Thank you, Joel, Don Milam, Tracy, and all the DI staff. There's a whole generation of people who need the enlightenment that you are called to bring. Thanks for the excellent work. Kathy Deering, you are a wordsmith and a woman of grace. I learned so much by working with you.

Dennis and Susan Freeman, Denny and Karen Freeman, and Rick Jones—thanks for your wisdom, support, and faith. Tom and Dorothy Caldwell, Angela and all the Caldwell Securities team—O'Canada. Go Canada.

Special thanks to all the saints who have believed, prayed for, and supported us. Without you this work could not have been done. Jim and Ramona Rickard, Mike and Sandy Smith, and all the tribes that have gathered in the twin cities—may the Lord take you beyond what we've seen. To Rich and Lindy Oliver for opening the gates for the river; we believe for the harvest with you. Todd and Joy and Gateway family, Chris and Dayna Varga—special grace for the new season. Believe all; believe big.

Finally, our Nashville friends, Bill and Noni Butler, Josh and Nita Ellis, The Glory Girls, Don Finto, Encounters Teams, Stacy Lawson, Grace Center and all the graced gatherings in Middle Earth Tenn—thank you!

There are so many more people and places...We carry all of you in our hearts and need your love, prayers, and support. The challenges we face are our opportunities for our faith. Let's press in to attain our prophetic destiny.

Gratefully, Mickey and Barbara Robinson

Endorsements

Bonnie and I treasure the friendship that we have shared with Mickey and Barbara Robinson for over 25 years. We have seen few who walk with such a zeal for God and His people. Mickey has an accurate encouraging word from God for every season, and these prophetic words have come to pass without fail whether for us or our flock. This book is a fruit of a life lived in the midst of tears and joy, full of revelation and anointing. May you receive the spirit of Jubilee this couple carries!

Drs. Mahesh and Bonnie Chavda
All Nations Church

Mickey is a prophetic encourager. Graced by the Holy Spirit with gifts of healing and revelation, Mickey inspires people to believe that, with God, all things are possible.

Mickey has traveled with me in ministry and has also been a primary speaker at many of our conferences. I've known him and his family for over 25 years. He loves God's Word, he loves the church, and he loves people in general. In a time where multitudes are oppressed by fear and disorientation, Mickey's ministry is an oasis of life and refreshing.

If you are seeking spiritual direction for your life, this ministry will help secure you on the path to God.

Francis Frangipane
Author, International Teacher, and Founder of
In Christ's Image Training (ICIT)

The Prophetic Made Personal by Mickey Robinson is definitely a book that you will want for your personal library. It will unlock potential in you, and it also offers balanced, practical teaching on growing and maturing in the prophetic gifting and unction as well as godly character. I love this book!

Patricia King
President and Founder of XPmedia.com
Author, Teacher, and TV Host of
Extreme Prophetic TV
www.pak@xpmedia.com
www.xpmedia.com

Our dear friend, Mickey Robinson, is one of the most passionate voices we know in the church today. He lives out his deep conviction to see the church fully equipped and the lost come to Jesus. This book is a clear explanation of what Scripture says about the prophetic, from one who has radically experienced the power of God. We are thankful for what we've learned from Mickey and are convinced you will be too!

Michael W. and Debbie Smith
Forerunners in Contemporary Christian Music,
Worship Leader, and Founder of
Rocket Town Youth Center, Nashville, TN

I read the book! It is balanced and fantastic! I can even hear his voice when I read it!

Rita Baloche
Songwriter, Worship Leader, Recording Artist

I personally know Mickey and have been fortunate to work with him at many conferences. Mickey's earnest, fervent love for God and His people is evident. Mickey continues to move in the prophetic gifts and passionately encourages and teaches about these gifts with great clarity. He is a true voice for this generation!

Paul Baloche
Songwriter, Worship Leader, Recording Artist

This is the book I have been looking for over the years: Christ-centered, biblical, pastoral, practical, and personal. It builds up the whole church, which is called to be prophetic. Robinson shows us, in the words of John Wimber, that "everybody gets to play." In fact, every Christian is already playing, although many don't know it. Prophecy is not a platform gift for an anointed few. Since Jesus' ministry was (and is) prophetic, we all are to follow His lead.

Robinson takes us on this journey, equipping the church, guiding us away from pitfalls and excesses and into the intimacy of hearing from the Lord, letting the Spirit lead, and doing what He says. The "Purpose-Driven Church" must become the "Prophecy-Driven Church," and Robinson shows us how. Get this book, read it, and go for it.

Don Williams, Ph.D.
Vineyard Pastor
Santa Monica, CA

Contents

Foreword

What I am about to do is one of the highest honors I have ever been given. Sounds odd, you say? I have been in full-time vocational ministry for well over 35 years. I have ministered on every continent and have written books that have been translated into over 20 languages. I have been interviewed on scores of television and radio shows and have written magazine articles for years. But this is one of my highest honors. "What is?" you quietly ponder.... Well, stay with me for a moment and you will understand.

How can you compose a foreword to a book called *The Prophetic Made Personal* if you did not personally know the author? That would really come off stale, religious, and actually kind of strange. What is my honor? It is my great privilege to compose a foreword for a book by a man of God who happens to be one of my best friends.

Recently at Mickey's 60th birthday party, I gave him a card that I trust touched his heart. It was a birthday card for a "brother." I have no brother in the natural, but I do in the spirit! Mickey Robinson is my brother! He lives life to the fullest, and he is a modern-day champion of the faith. I know! He's my brother!

Mickey embodies his message. Mickey doesn't just bubble up and pop up and spout off his latest revelation. He is a revelation! He is a word from God made personal. If you know him—you love him. If you have been with him—you leave encouraged, charged in your faith, and ready to find a bear, a lion, something to pick a fight with, and win!

In the hours of my trial and pain, Mickey and his dear wife, Barbara, have been my constant source of camaraderie. For years they have been some of the closest friends to both Michal Ann and myself. They loved my wife, Michal Ann, and I love them for that. Friends play together, laugh together, and go to war together. The Robinsons and the Golls have done just that. We have done the conference circuit together and then gone to "chill," forgetting the dog-eat-dog religious circles and simply going to the movies!

So you think that this is just another book on the prophetic... Do we really need another book? Yes, we need this one! Mickey is the master artist of earthing out a prophetic word. The Robinsons lives always testify of Jesus! They live it through their actions, their worship, their family, their miraculous impartation, and their capacity to rebound for the Gospel's sake! They are the Comeback Kids!

Want a word made sure? Want to sharpen your prophetic senses? Want training that is practical, accessible, and yet pushes you to do the impossible? Then devour this book in your hands. *The Prophetic Made Personal* is not just another book to be added to the revelatory arsenal of our day. This book should be the foundation upon which everything else proceeds!

Charged with Faith!

James W. Goll
Encounters Network, Prayer Storm, Compassion Acts,
Author of *The Seer, The Lost Art of Intercession,
Dream Language, Angelic Encounters, The Coming Israel
Awakening,* and many more

Introduction
Jesus, the Model Prophet

The big-name prophets—Jeremiah, Isaiah, Daniel, Elijah, Ezekiel—speak in the pages of the Old Testament, as do plenty of other prophets who are also familiar to us: Hosea, Joel, Amos, Obadiah, Jonah, Micah, Nahum, Habakkuk, Zephaniah, Haggai, Zechariah, Malachi, Elisha, and dozens more.

Yet all of them put together can only point to the greatest prophet of all—Jesus Christ:

> *In the past God spoke to our forefathers through the prophets at many times and in various ways, but in these last days He has spoken to us by His Son...*[who is] *the radiance of God's glory and the exact representation of His being...* (Hebrews 1:1-3 NIV).

In the New Testament, only one book (the Book of Revelation) is considered prophetic. In the rest of the books, only a few prophets are mentioned. Philip had four daughters who were prophetesses (see Acts 21:8-9).

Not much else is said about them. Agabus was a notable prophet who prophesied about the famine in Jerusalem, a crisis for which the community needed to provide a remedy (see Acts 11:28). Later, he also performed a prophetic gesture and handcuffed himself with Paul's belt. "This is what is going to happen to the man who owns this belt if he goes to Jerusalem" (see Acts 21:10-11).

Paul writes, *"I was appointed a preacher and an apostle...a teacher"* (1 Tim. 2:7), yet his entire ministry was ignited and guided by extraordinary prophetic revelation, as were many of the other servant leaders named in the New Testament. Judas and Silas traveled with Barnabas and Paul on their missionary journeys. Later, after the important council in Jerusalem, they were entrusted to deliver a letter to the Gentile churches. The Bible states that *"Judas and Silas, also being prophets themselves, encouraged and strengthened the brethren with a lengthy message"* (Acts 15:32). Yet as significant as this was, not one of the things they said in their message was quoted in the Bible nor is any description of them portrayed.

None of these New Testament prophets exemplify everything about being a prophet. The only one who does that is Jesus Christ. He is the One we need to pay attention to. The model prophet for a Christian is Jesus Christ. The other prophets look to His Spirit for everything they say.

Under the Old Covenant, the Spirit anointed certain people at certain times. With the advent of the New Covenant, the Spirit became available to everybody all the time.

God spoke through one of the Old Testament prophets, declaring, *"...I will pour out My Spirit on all flesh..."* (Joel 2:28 NKJV). Through His Son Jesus, He fulfilled that word. Jesus told the people:

If anyone is thirsty, let him come to Me and drink. He who believes in Me, as the Scripture said, "From his innermost being will flow rivers of living water." But this He spoke of the Spirit, whom those who believed in Him were to receive; for the Spirit was not yet given, because Jesus was not yet glorified (John 7:37-39).

After Jesus was glorified, at last that promise was fulfilled on the day of Pentecost (see Acts 2). He breathed His Spirit into the people and created the Body of the Church.

That promise, by the way, has no expiration date. Nowhere in Scripture or in the experience of the Church throughout history is there any indication that Jesus would send His Holy Spirit only for a specified period of time (for instance, until the last apostle died), and then the Spirit would leave the world. Where did people get the idea of a limited dispensation of the Holy Spirit—that He would come to help the new Church gain some momentum and then decide to leave because His people would be fully equipped to handle it from then on?

That mistaken notion has been our demise, hasn't it? Every time God starts something new, like children, we say, "OK, Father, we can do it all by ourselves now." Then we write books and build monuments to the people who had the real experience with God's Spirit, but we are only reporting what happened. We are not living it ourselves anymore. We do not understand that God wants to keep pouring out His Spirit on all flesh.

You see, the whole subject of the prophetic lifestyle begins and ends with the revelation of God Himself, as continually shown to us by His Spirit in the life of His Son, Jesus. It is always happening, and it is always personal.

Has the gift of prophecy been abused? Of course. Hasn't there also been abuse of the written Word of God? Have we seen valid prophetic ministry from gifted people right alongside abuse of the same? Without a doubt. Does that mean we should throw it all out? Of course not.

Instead of finding fault and throwing stones, let's just learn to do it right. The right kind of prophetic ministry, when it is really God, has so much grace and beauty. Instead of shutting it down and ignoring it, let's revive it and wake people up. Instead of being intimidated into passivity, let's throw off the spirit of heaviness and return both to our first love (the Lord Jesus) and our high calling as His representatives on the Earth today.

Instead of talking about the negative potential for the gift of prophecy, let's talk about the benefits of being in a personal relationship with the Shepherd—the One who said, *"My sheep hear My voice..."* (John 10:27). Are you one of His sheep? Are you communing with Him? He wants to talk to you as much as you ever want to talk to Him.

Prophecy, the Cornerstone Gift

I believe that prophecy is the cornerstone gift of the Church. It was through this gift that Simon Peter, who is one of the primary "living stones" in the foundation of the Church, declared who Jesus was.

Jesus liked to ask His disciples questions. One day He asked them, *"Who do people say that the Son of Man is?"* (Matt. 16:13). They told Him that people seemed to think He was John the Baptist raised from the dead or one of the prophets—Jeremiah or Elijah. Then Jesus asked them, *"But who do you say that I am?"* (Matt. 16:15). There was a hush. Then Simon Peter took a step forward, and in a moment of supernatural inspiration, he said, *"You are the Christ, the Son of the living God"* (Matt. 16:16).

> *And Jesus said to him, "Blessed are you, Simon Barjona, because flesh and blood did not reveal this to you, but My Father who is in heaven. I also say to you that you are Peter, and upon this rock I will build My church; and the gates of Hades will not overpower it"* (Matthew 16:17-18).

Jesus was making a personal prophetic declaration about Peter's personal prophetic destiny. Jesus wanted the other disciples to know that Peter had spoken out loud what the Holy Spirit had revealed to him.

By and large, Peter scored well in the prophecy department. But like most of us, he also had some startlingly low points, such as immediately after his declaration above, when Jesus started to talk about being killed, and he blurted out, *"God forbid it, Lord! This shall never happen to You"* (Matt. 16:22). Jesus then turned to him and said, *"Get behind Me, Satan! You are a stumbling block to Me; for you are not setting your mind on God's interests, but man's"* (Matt. 16:23).

What a contrast! Was this the same person?

If you have read the whole story, you know that Peter did not crash and burn on that one—nor did he give up permanently after the crucifixion when he denied that he even knew the Lord (see Matt. 26:74-75). Peter found his way back, thanks to the Lord. After Jesus died and rose again, He paid a special visit to Peter (see John 21). He wanted to restore him in every way so that he could live the rest of his life as God's friend.

That night, Peter and several of the other disciples had gone fishing. Although Peter had seen that Jesus had been raised from the dead, he did not consider himself worthy to be a disciple, so he returned to his former vocation as a fisherman. With Jesus gone, he and the others had not known what else to do. Although they were professional fishermen who knew their business well, that night had not been a good one for them. They had fished through all the hours of darkness, and now at dawn they were hauling in their empty nets. Peter was probably muttering to himself. "Nothing is going right anymore. No fish, no paycheck. We dragged these nets up one side of Lake Galilee and down the other. On top of being a failure as a disciple, I'm now a failure as a fisherman."

Just then, an unidentified lone figure on the beach called out to them, "Hey, did you catch anything?"

"No," they replied.

The mysterious inquirer, as if he knew something they didn't, told them to throw their nets over the starboard side of the boat. *Well, sure. OK. What did they have to lose?* Instantaneously, they caught so many flopping fish that they could hardly manage the net, a repeat of the same type of miracle that Jesus performed when He initially called Peter and prophetically declared his destiny (see Luke 5:1-11). Peter suddenly recognized that it was *Jesus* who had spoken to them from the shore. He plunged into the water and swam ashore to greet Him.

It was over a breakfast of fish, through a series of more questions, that the Lord re-established Peter's relationship with Him, and commissioned him to carry on feeding His sheep (His people) and fulfilling his original call. When He had first summoned him as a disciple, He had said, *"Follow Me, and I will make you fishers of men"* (Matt. 4:19; Mark 1:17). Now humble and reliant on the Holy Spirit, Peter would be able to do it.

Peter's life is a story about personal prophecy—with compound interest. You and I are Peter's fellow disciples, and hearing about his experience can help us.

The Revelation of Jesus Christ

You see, *everything* points to Jesus. The number one prophetic revelation is the revelation of Jesus Christ. "The Revelation of Jesus Christ" is also the full name of the last book of the Bible, and it is the first phrase of the first verse in it:

> *The Revelation of Jesus Christ, which God gave Him to show His servants—things which must shortly take place. And He sent and signified it by His angel to His servant John, who bore witness to the word of God, and to the testimony of Jesus Christ, to all things that he saw* (Revelation 1:1-2 NKJV).

The Book of Revelation is an extraordinary book, and it has incited a lot of strong opinions. Putting aside the spectacular parts and people's reactions to them, the book is simply about the revelation of Jesus Christ. It is the detailed uncovering of His majesty, His power, His personality, and what it means for us to believe in Him. Definitively, it shows us that Jesus Christ is the only model to follow. He is Number One in every category, including the category of "prophet."

If you want to obey prophecy, you will do everything that He says. If you want to honor the Lord Jesus Christ, you will listen to His voice. By listening to His voice and following Him, you will be changed into a person who resembles Him. As you become more like Him, you will be able to represent Him to others. Then you will be able to express His message in words and deeds—which means that you too will become increasingly more prophetic. You will become a person who "reads the red." You will be one who pays attention to every word that Jesus says, whether it has been printed in red ink in your Bible or whether He just whispered it to you this morning. He will tell you things, and He will tell you what to do with His words. One of the Lord's beautiful promises to us is: *"The Helper, the Holy Spirit, whom the Father will send in My name, He will teach you all things, and bring to your remembrance all that I said to you"* (John 14:26).

Although we may understand that God has established certain individuals as prophets in the Church, too few of us consider ourselves to be in their league. In this book, I want to open up the way for every person to enter into new and fulfilling prophetic possibilities, providing plenty of biblical and historical background for the operation of prophetic gifts as I also explain safeguards and practical methods for prophetic ministry. The operation of prophetic gifts should be as natural as breathing—because we are filled to overflowing with the Holy Spirit, who is the breath of God.

Chapter 1

You Are Prophetic

The prophetic ministry has been misperceived as a strange, elitist ministry. This is because it appears to be the offbeat domain of spiritual specialists. God's word has also too often been presented with sensational hyping, misleading communication, and other unfortunate elements. As a result, "prophecy" has lost credibility.

To counter this misrepresentation, let me underscore these two facts: *the prophetic ministry is about personal relationship with our Lord Jesus Christ* and *God wants to pour out His Spirit on **all** flesh.* If there is anything that is inclusive about God, it is the gifts of revelation. Many of us experience them for years without realizing what they are. They came to us as part of the promise. Once we were born again of the Spirit of God, we began to feel the wind of the Spirit (see John 3:8).

Prophetic, revelatory experiences are for everybody. Whoever belongs to Jesus communicates with Him, spirit-to-Spirit, in a variety of ways. Think back about your own life. Can you see how He has communicated with you? You may not have heard an audible, theatrical voice from Heaven, but you can see ways in which He has directed you, protected you, or assured you that He cares about you.

As long as you keep following Him, you will be learning more about hearing His voice and following His direction. You will also grow in your understanding of the place of prophetic expression in the house of the Lord and in personal ministry. Your prophetic education will occur in practical ways as the Lord guides you through your daily life, showing you Scripture and giving you tastes of the ways He expresses Himself.

It is a fact: whoever you are and wherever you live and work, you are a prophet and priest in the Kingdom of God (see 1 Pet. 2:9).

Dispensations of Grace

Over the eons, God has dispensed His grace in different ways. At the Creation, God expressed Himself directly and magnificently. Then the dispensation of His grace changed under the Old Covenant relationship between God and humans. For thousands of years, He expressed Himself through particular individuals. The prophetic anointing was relegated to certain prophets and kings who were set apart. God rested on them when they prophesied. Ordinary people did not have this experience at all. And there were long stretches when the word of the Lord was rare (see 1 Sam. 3:1).

Then Jesus came, and He ushered in a brand-new dispensation of grace. From Pentecost on, every believer could share in the anointing because God's Holy Spirit was dwelling in every one of them. Today we are living in a time of a particular operation of God's grace and sovereign activity that is a continuation of the New Testament.

All of these manifestations represent the same God because they show us different expressions of His nature. They do not erase and replace each other; they build on each other. The Old Testament is just as relevant today as the New Testament.

To appreciate the Old Testament revelation as much as New Testament revelation, just look at the Book of Hebrews, which is like an elegant bridgework connecting the former dispensation with the new:

> *God, after He spoke long ago to the fathers in the prophets in many portions and in many ways, in these last days has spoken to us in His Son, whom He appointed heir of all things, through whom also He made the world. And He is the radiance of His glory and the exact representation of His nature, and upholds all things by the word of His power. When He had made purification of sins, He sat down at the right hand of the Majesty on high (Hebrews 1:1-3).*

The Old Testament emphasis on the Law has not been replaced; it has been fulfilled. With fresh eyes, you can read both testaments and you can say, "This is what it really means. All of it has been leading us to God." All that God created is being held together by the Word of God, who has been speaking since the beginning of time and who is still speaking today.

"My Sheep Hear My Voice"

In your relationship with God, *you have to be prophetic.* The Word makes it clear that *"all who are being led by the Spirit of God, these are sons of God"* (Rom. 8:14), and *"...it is He who has made us, and not we ourselves; we are His people and the sheep of His pasture"* (Ps. 100:3).

If you are being led by the Spirit of God, you have communication with Him. If you are one of the *"sheep of His pasture,"* you will know His voice when you hear it. When Jesus said, *"My sheep hear My voice..."* (John 10:27), it was not just a sweet metaphor. Real sheep have it figured out. They know the difference between their shepherd's voice and other voices.

One time I was in Israel. I was near a well on a hillside outside of Bethlehem, where the terrain is arid. A shepherd had just taken the cover off the well so that he could draw water for his flock. A friend was with me, and he said he had been at the same spot another time when a very large flock of sheep had been milling around, grazing on the sparse, brownish-green tufts, thirsty. A man had come up to them and made a particular sound. It was a loud, guttural sound, not even a real word. Half of the sheep looked up and took off to gather around him, but the other half of the sheep never even moved. They just kept their heads down, scrounging around in the dust. Then another man came along and made a different kind of a distinct sound. Those sheep knew that one. They raised their heads en masse and began to follow him.

You see, the sheep knew the voice of their *own* shepherd. They would not follow the wrong one. Their ears had been trained to recognize a particular voice, and as far as they were concerned, the other voice was just a noise to be ignored. They would not go with the wrong shepherd because his voice sounded counterfeit to them. Lambs follow other sheep; sheep know and follow the voice of The Shepherd.

We are the sheep of Jesus' pasture through the New Covenant in His blood (see 1 Cor. 11:25). Jesus Himself is the Shepherd, the Head of the Church. The collective "flock" is made up of individual people. The Lord takes care of the whole Church by taking care of individual members of it. Each one of us can expect to hear His voice for ourselves, even as we move in concert with others who also hear His voice.

"Would God That All the Lord's People Were Prophets!"

In the Book of Joel, we find the line that Peter used on the day of Pentecost to explain how the Spirit was going to be poured out on every individual who would say yes to Jesus:

> *It will come about after this that I will pour out My Spirit on all mankind; and your sons and daughters will prophesy, your old men will dream dreams, your young men will see visions. Even on the male and female servants I will pour out My Spirit in those days* (Joel 2:28-29).

In the context of Joel's time, this was a revolutionary statement. In those days the blessing of the Spirit was reserved for a select few people, with very few exceptions. One of the exceptions had occurred with Moses and the 70 elders:

> *Moses went out and told the people the words of the Lord. Also, he gathered seventy men of the elders of the people, and stationed them around the tent. Then the Lord came down in the cloud and spoke to him; and He took of the Spirit who was upon him and placed Him upon the seventy elders. And when the Spirit rested upon them, they prophesied. But they did not do it again.*
>
> *But two men had remained in the camp; the name of one was Eldad and the name of the other Medad. And the Spirit rested upon them (now they*

were among those who had been registered, but had not gone out to the tent), and they prophesied in the camp. So a young man ran and told Moses and said, "Eldad and Medad are prophesying in the camp."

Then Joshua the son of Nun, the attendant of Moses from his youth, said, "Moses, my lord, restrain them."

But Moses said to him, **"Are you jealous for my sake? Would that all the Lord's people were prophets, that the Lord would put His Spirit upon them"** (Numbers 11:24-29).

Moses was tired of being the only one who could hear from God. He knew that it was good to hear from God, and he also knew that it would change anyone who heard His voice. If all of God's people could be prophets, what a wonderful day that would be.

When you hear the voice of the Lord, it will fill you with awe and healthy fear. It will straighten you up. When you hear God speak to you, His voice will stand you up—and lay you down—in the same motion. It will strengthen you as it humbles you. The fear of the Lord is the accurate moral, spiritual, and relational compass.

So when God's Spirit was poured out as never before on Pentecost, Peter referred back to those early prophecies. What happened on the day of Pentecost fulfilled Joel's prophecy in living color. One hundred and twenty ordinary-looking folks were speaking fluently in languages they could never have learned—declaring the truth, proclaiming the Kingdom of God. Thousands of people came running to find out what was going on, whereupon Peter began to preach an amazing sermon, fulfilling the prophetic word that had been spoken about his becoming a fisher of men. After Peter's explanation, they gave their own altar call, saying, "What are we supposed to do now?" (see Acts 2:37). That day, 3,000 "fish" came into the Kingdom after hearing only one sermon.

This was supposed to continue on through the centuries. In one way or another, it has. But along the way, most of the Church lost the theology of the Holy Spirit, in part because it was abused by people who had strayed from the heart of the issue.

Our Response to This Dispensation of Grace

To get back what we have lost, all we need is a heart to hear and a will to obey. I think it was Vince Lombardi who said, "Winning isn't everything. It's the only thing." We in the Church should change that statement to this one: "Hearing from God isn't everything. It's the only thing."

Hearing from someone is the basis of relationship. What kind of a relationship would it be if you called your spouse or your friend and you did all of the talking and the other person could not get a word in edgewise? Not only would you fail to engage in a real conversation, but also probably the other person would soon tune you out.

To have a healthy relationship with God and to gain from it, you cannot be passive. You need to incline your heart in His direction, believing that He has something to say to you. This familiar proverb applies:

> *My son, if you will receive my words and treasure my commandments within you, make your ear attentive to wisdom, incline your heart to understanding; for if you cry for discernment, lift your voice for understanding; if you seek her as silver and search for her as for hidden treasures; then you will discern the fear of the Lord and discover the knowledge of God* (Proverbs 2:1-5).

To say it another way, you have to learn how to incline your ear to Him in order to have a relationship with God:

Listen, O daughter, give attention and incline your ear: forget your people and your father's house; then the King will desire your beauty. Because He is your Lord, bow down to Him (Psalm 45:10-11).

Once you incline yourself toward Him, you are more inclined to obey what He tells you. Once you get used to hearing Him, you will get better at obedient accountability and discover, as I have, that *dis*obedience carries no rewards at all, except as a prod to seek His grace to obey Him next time. Your reward for obedience will be an abundantly joy-filled life.

Hearing God is a supernatural thing, and you need His grace to both hear and obey. You need to sharpen the capacity of your perception with constant use. You have probably been doing it already, but I want to encourage you to do it more. With God there is always more.

God Calls You to Do the Impossible

God will rarely tell you what you already know, and He will rarely call you to do what you already can do by your own strength. I know that does not sound very encouraging, but it is true.

The reason, again, is *relationship*—God wants you to cultivate a relationship with Him, and it must be a relationship built on trust and faith. You cannot live on somebody else's faith, and you cannot live on the faith you operated in last year. You need to maintain ongoing communication back and forth. You need to talk to Him (which is prayer—breathing out) and then you need to listen when He talks to you (which is prophecy—breathing in).

You may not hear His audible voice. Neither will He preface every word with "Thus saith the Lord." Sometimes, just as in any relationship, He will communicate with a sigh or the equivalent of a lifted eyebrow. Increasingly, you will learn what His voice sounds like. You will learn how to wait for Him before you do something, and you will also learn to respond immediately when He tells you what to do. Sometimes what He says will not seem to make any sense, especially if He uses figurative terms. Other times what He tells you will make so much sense that it will melt your heart. He is a God of wonders and a God of wisdom, and He wants to share His abundance with you.

As a result of hearing and obeying, you *will* be stretched. You will be inconvenienced. You may even be persecuted. But it will be worth it.

What do you think it was like for the early Church when the persecutions started? They had been enjoying phenomenal growth and remarkable harmony. Except for the shocking deaths of Ananias and Sapphira and a few reprimands and beatings from the authorities, thousands of people were getting healed, sharing their lives with each other, and spreading the Good News:

> *And the congregation of those who believed were of one heart and soul; and not one of them claimed that anything belonging to him was his own, but all things were common property to them. And with great power the apostles were giving testimony to the resurrection of the Lord Jesus, and abundant grace was upon them all.*

> *...The word of God kept on spreading; and the number of the disciples continued to increase greatly in Jerusalem, and a great many of the priests were becoming obedient to the faith* (Acts 4:32-33; 6:7).

Then the gifted deacon named Stephen was stoned to death, and *"on that day a great persecution began against the church in Jerusalem, and they were all scattered throughout the regions of Judea and Samaria, except the apostles"* (Acts 8:1).

That single line cannot portray what it must have been like for the individuals and families who had to drop everything and flee for their lives. Because of the persecution and forced dispersion, however, the Gospel message spread far and wide, and before long the Church of Jesus Christ even embraced Gentiles. The believers kept on believing, praying, and obeying in the grace and power of the Holy Spirit.

Saul of Tarsus, one of the worst persecutors and probably the last person you would think would be converted, was. And his story gives us another glimpse into how much the members of the new Church listened to God's voice. An ordinary brother, also named Ananias (but apparently no relation to the other one) received a prophetic word from God:

> *Now there was a disciple at Damascus named Ananias; and the Lord said to him in a vision, "Ananias." And he said, "Here I am, Lord." And the Lord said to him, "Get up and go to the street called Straight, and inquire at the house of Judas for a man from Tarsus named Saul, for he is praying, and he has seen in a vision a man named Ananias come in and lay his hands on him, so that he might regain his sight."*
>
> *But Ananias answered, "Lord, I have heard from many about this man, how much harm he did to Your saints at Jerusalem; and here he has authority from the chief priests to bind all who call on Your name."*

But the Lord said to him, "Go, for he is a chosen instrument of Mine, to bear My name before the Gentiles and kings and the sons of Israel; for I will show him how much he must suffer for My name's sake."

So Ananias departed and entered the house, and after laying his hands on him said, "Brother Saul, the Lord Jesus, who appeared to you on the road by which you were coming, has sent me so that you may regain your sight and be filled with the Holy Spirit."

And immediately there fell from his eyes some-thing like scales, and he regained his sight, and he got up and was baptized (Acts 9:10-18).

Do you see how important it was for Ananias to be able to receive prophetic input from God? He had to be willing to obey in the face of risk, too, didn't he? What God told him to do sounded impossible for several rea-sons. But he heard accurately and obeyed anyway.

That is radical faith, which to me seems harder than going into a strange neighborhood and doing cold-calling evangelism, knocking on strangers' doors. But Ananias heard from God, and he knew he was being sent.

Whatever Jesus says to you, do it. Do not ask too many questions, and do not hesitate out of fear. The few words that Mary spoke to the servants at the wedding in Cana should become our motto: *"Whatever He says to you, do it"* (John 2:5).

God Will Make a Miracle

Just as Jesus did when He turned plain water into fine wine at Cana, He will start with something as common as *you* and make a miracle out of you. In every creative miracle, Jesus used something common, whether He spit on the ground to make mud or accepted two fish and five barley loaves. He said something for somebody to respond to, and He made a miracle through the interaction.

Just as it was in Cana or Jerusalem, this common thing turned creative miracle may seem like a divine interruption. It was not part of your Plan A. But if you have been listening for God's voice all along, you will recognize it and obey it, even if He is nudging you out of your comfort zone.

Let me give you a personal example. A few years ago, I was in the Atlanta airport waiting for a connecting flight. I had enough time to go get something to eat, so I found a restaurant by my gate, which the ticket agent had told me was A3. The place was packed, with a line of people out the door. As soon as I got there, I realized that the agent had made a small mistake—I was supposed to be at A33. Now I was a man in a serious hurry! I spotted one empty barstool, so I asked the hostess if I could sit there and she said OK. So I sat down and ordered. Whew. I was sitting next to a lady who was having a sandwich. She looked nice and she appeared to be about 60. As I ate, I was trying to catch the football scores on CNN and also make a phone call to make sure that somebody was going to be able to pick me up when I landed. The Holy Spirit broke through all the noise in my head and said, "Ask her what she's doing."

I did not really feel I had enough time, but I said, "Hello, what are you doing?" Her answer was, "Well, I am going to see my daughter who lives in California. I was married for 30 years and my husband was in the military. We lived all over the world. A few months ago he told me he never loved me and that all of those years he's had a mistress. Now we're divorced and we sold everything and he's retired. He's going to live in South America, but I don't know where I'm going to go."

Her whole world had completely fallen apart, shattered and devastated. I said the first thing that occurred to me, "Ma'am, God sent me to tell you that He loves you," and in 90 seconds I shared my testimony about how God had mercy on me when I was in an accident. (She could tell from looking at me that it was no small accident.) Then I said to her, "What happened to you is not an accident. God is going to take care of you. Jesus loves you." I gave her a printed copy of my testimony, and I showed her the phone number in case she wanted to call me later. She was bawling, and her mascara was running down and staining her beautiful sweater.

That was all I had time for. I had to get up and leave if I was going to catch my plane. I was crying too, by then. I do not know how her situation turned out, but I do know I was able to give her some hope and a lifeline.

God used a short layover and a mistake about the gate—and a quick prophetic word—to make a difference in someone's life. It could happen more often if we were open to it.

The good news is that God is loving and merciful, and He wants our attention. We are His servants, and He needs to be able to tell us what to do. Sometimes I think He goes to all these lengths to interrupt us and inconvenience us not only to get us to do things, but also to condition us to be listening for His voice.

God Calls You as Part of His Church

As individuals, we are part of a prophetic servant community called the Church. Here again, Jesus is our model. He called Himself the servant of all, so we are servants serving Jesus, the Servant of All (see John 13:12-16). Although

Jesus is the King of kings and the Lord of lords, He came to serve men and women and to be a servant leader. Even if you think you have a big personal ministry, the biggest and greatest ministry is to be the servant of all.

With Him as our example, we are humble fellow-servants, working together for a common purpose and under the prophetic guidance of God, serving as the Holy Spirit leads us. Even with the highest motives, we should not pour ourselves out aimlessly to the point of exhaustion. We need to be directed by God, and we need to obey, both individually and together.

The Bible calls us *"living stones"* who are being built together into a spiritual house, *"to offer up spiritual sacrifices acceptable to God through Jesus Christ"* (1 Pet. 2:5). Each of us has a divinely appointed destiny, and it includes being built together with others. As we encounter others, we will be transformed, together, into Christlikeness, and we will mature in our ability to live lives that are submitted to Him.

Our message to the world will not come only in the form of the spoken or written word. For the most part, it will come in the form of our transformed lives and the powerful love of God demonstrated through signs and wonders. The Kingdom of God is both a declaration and a demonstration.

Here is another example from the early Church. The apostles in Jerusalem had sent Barnabas up to Antioch to help out. The account shows that he listened to the Lord all the time; the good results of his visit prove it.

> *When he arrived and witnessed the grace of God, he rejoiced and began to encourage them all with resolute heart to remain true to the Lord; for he was a good man, and full of the Holy Spirit and of faith. And considerable numbers were brought to*

the Lord (Acts 11:23-24).

After a short time, Barnabas went to Tarsus and located Paul and brought him to Antioch, *"and for an entire year they met with the church and taught considerable numbers; and the disciples were first called Christians in Antioch"* (Acts 11:26).

Most people have been told that Barnabas' name means "son of encouragement," which comes from the Greek version of his name. But really, in his native Aramaic it is closer to "son of prophecy" (*Bar* means "son of" and *nabas* means "prophet").

Barnabas made a habit of inclining his heart to hear God's voice, and he was so successful at bringing God's life to the new believers in Antioch that the unbelievers began to call them "Christians," or "little Christs." The citizens of Antioch did not call the believers "the group from Jerusalem" or "the group of Jews and Greeks." They observed their lifestyle, and they saw that these people did all the things that Jesus had done, and they did them in His name. They preached, they prayed, they prophesied, they laid hands on the sick and healed them, they spoke words of life, they loved each other. They were just like Jesus. They were a prophetic servant community expressing the love, power, and passion of God.

I want to be part of something like that, don't you? I want to be able to be part of a courageous and loving body of people that blesses everybody. It is not too strong to say that I want to be an incarnation of my Lord Jesus Christ, just as those early disciples in Antioch were.

To do that, I need to be a prophetic servant. I need to be learning more about hearing the voice of God as I do what He tells me to do. I need to learn how to be humble and submitted to Him and to other people. And I want you to join me!

A Sending Prayer

Lord, we have tasted and seen that You are good. There is something that is burning in us that is compelling us to express Your love, to spread Your Kingdom, to bring others into a full relationship with You. Something leaps up in our spirits when we hear that each one of us is supposed to be a *prophet* in Your Kingdom.

Your Holy Spirit fills our hearts and makes us incline our spiritual ears to hear Your quiet voice. We turn our hearts and attention to You. We want You to become our Shepherd, our Guide, our Protector. We want to learn to recognize Your voice in the midst of many other voices competing for our attention. We want to obey You quickly and completely. Right now we activate our faith, and we ask You to help us to activate our ability to hear You so that we can really be living stones, individuals who are part of Your Church and who continually pulse with Your living Spirit. Amen.

Chapter 2

Releasing the Prophetic Church

In my life, you might say, I dove into the prophetic in a spectacular way. As you may already know if you have heard my testimony or read my book, *Falling to Heaven*, I was a skydiver, and I was almost killed in a horrific plane crash. My broken, burned body was pulled out just in time, and I spent the next five and a half years in the hospital and in recovery.

One day early on, when I was more dead than alive, my spirit came out of my physical body, and I went instantly into the spiritual realm. Without being told, I knew that this spiritual world is the real world and that my spiritual man is the real man. The colors were vivid. I had a complete awareness, not of time, because time is measured only in the physical realm, but of *eternity*.

I was traveling somewhere. I began to perceive that a great emptiness and blackness was closing around me. It was like someone was closing the door in a dark room and there was only a crack of light. This was not good. This was a total vacuum, an utter absence, and I knew it would last for eternity. No form of light, no sound, no movement. The blackness kept closing down until there was only about a half-inch of the pure white light left.

I began to cry out in my spirit just as I had when they brought me into the emergency room: "God, I am sorry! Give me another chance!" This big-shot, sky-diving superstar who could extricate himself from anything could not get out of this predicament by himself. Athletic talent, daring, money, good looks, charisma—nothing would suffice here. As soon as I began to cry out to this beautiful pure white light—I was *in* it.

I don't know where I was, but I was in the light. I cannot report that I visited the streets of New Jerusalem or that I saw any saints, but what I did see was the glory of God. And I can tell you that in His presence *is* fullness of joy and in His right hand are pleasures forevermore (see Ps. 16:11). His glory was like liquid golden radiation, vibrating forever in front of me, above me, below me, behind me. It went through me; it held everything together. This pulsating, powerful emanation radiated and shimmered with all of God's love, all of His power, all of His authority, all of His majesty. I knew that this God was going to take care of me forever.

I wanted to stay right there, but I knew I was going to have a future on Earth because I started to see things that were going to happen in the years to come. I saw people I did not know yet. I saw my wife, Barbara, before I had ever met her. I saw how the drug scene in America would unfold and the horrors that it would bring. I saw years of time in an instant.

Then, without explanation, I was headed back to Earth. The same way that I had gotten there, I was traveling back through space, time, and realms of the spirit world back into Earth's dimension. As my spirit settled into my physical body, I could actually feel my spirit pushing through my flesh. (Imagine what it would feel like to be the wind blowing through a big bushy tree with leaves on it; that's what it felt like.) I began to see out of my eye (only one of them worked) and hear through my ears again, and I heard myself speaking this incredible language. My 106-degree fever broke, and for the first time I lay my head down and fell asleep. When I woke up I felt as if I were on a raft, floating on an ocean of peace. With the big medical apparatus around me and the very uptight doctors and nurses looking at me, I was just held in this stunning peace.

I was still a very sick young man, pretty much a goner—one notch up from roadkill. I was blind in one eye and both legs were paralyzed. I had a brain injury, and my esophagus had a hole in it. The medical staff was worried, very serious, measuring, checking, waiting for me to die.

Fast forward a bit. About a month later, I was still as sick as a dog. They had evacuated the intensive care unit because another patient had gotten a staph infection; and if I had become infected, it would have killed me. They set me up in a kind of makeshift ICU on the first floor. One day, this guy was cruising down the hall with his Bible, and he wound up in my room. He introduced himself, but I couldn't remember his name, and he asked if he could pray for me. He prayed for me, but I don't remember a word of what he said. Then he asked if he could read the Bible to me. I said OK.

When he started reading the Bible (I don't know what part), something began to shake in my stomach. As soon as he started to speak out the Word, I began to vibrate. The metal bars on the sides of the bed were clanging against the frame of the bed because I was vibrating so violently. Inside of me, a word was building up, and then, like a volcano, I burst out with, "I have got to be some kind of a priest or something. I have been reborn." Now this was before Christian television, and nothing in my background had provided me with the idea of being "born again."

The guy said, "Just take it easy. Just slow down, would you? I'm going to get a nurse. You quiet down. Don't worry about this stuff now." And he took off. This poor man thought he had gotten me too worked up. I never saw him again.

What had really happened was that when the Word of the Lord was read, the Spirit of God in me got excited and out of my mouth came a prophecy. It did not go through my brain. It just rose up from inside when the Spirit heard the Word. And even though I still had to go through medical torture to get well enough to leave the hospital, that prophetic word was the truth. Today I *am* "some kind of a priest or something."

During my long recovery and rehabilitation, I did not know anybody I could talk to about this. Primarily I was concerned with getting better, but throughout this time, I was learning about my relationship with God. He would speak to me, and I knew it was Him. I thought it was normal for people to be able to hear the Lord like this, but I didn't have any perspective on it.

But I want you to know that I really was not that useful to Him at that point. Not until I got into a church did I become useful to Him.

You Must Have a Place

I believe that there are lots of people who have amazing experiences with the Lord as individuals, but they are not very useful to the Lord and His Kingdom simply because they are not in a place where they can be used. We must have a *place*. We have to operate in the context of the local church.

In chapter 12 of Paul's first letter to the Corinthians, he pictures the Church as a human body with various organs and parts. This is as true today as it was when he wrote it. Each of us is one of the component parts of the Body of Christ. Together we can function. Separated from each other, each one of us is little more than a lab specimen.

You need the other parts of the Body of Christ. If you are a prophet, you may be a "mouth," but you will not be able to speak the words that God gives you without the collaboration of all of the parts of the mouth—tongue, teeth, lips—not to mention the rest of the Body, without which you will not amount to much. That may be over-simplified, but it is true.

The local church is not a Sunday-only meeting. It is not an audience for a performance. It is a living organism where we give and receive the Holy Spirit. God does not want you to waste time comparing yourself to other people, coveting their gifts. He will help you find out who you are supposed to be, and He will help you develop in the context of the Church. Find your place within the Body of believers so you can begin to give and receive.

Joel's prophecy that was fulfilled on the day of Pentecost predicted that every single person would be filled with the Spirit. *"...I will pour out My Spirit on all mankind; and your sons and daughters will prophesy..."* (Joel 2:28). As you know, this fulfillment became the beginning of the Church. Never before in the dispensation of God had His Spirit been given this freely and generously, thus beginning and fulfilling of what Jesus had prophesied (quoting the prophet Isaiah), *"He who believes in Me, as the Scripture said, 'From his innermost being will flow rivers of living water'"*(John 7:38).

Now every individual has an inexhaustible supply of the water of the Spirit. Is it so that each person can build a fence around him- or herself and live happily ever after? Of course not. The outpouring of the Spirit created something new—a body of people held together by nothing but the love of God.

Indwelt with His Spirit, they learn to move with Him together. Separated from each other, the living water stagnates and turns to sludge. Together they can explore Kingdom life and introduce others to it. Apart they are like seeds carelessly sown by mistake alongside the road, in the gravel, or among thorns (see Matt. 13:1-9). Together they can give and receive, flowing with the Spirit of God, sharpening and improving their use of the spiritual gifts that the Spirit bestows on each person. Apart they would never know the rich comprehensiveness of their Father's provision here on Earth.

Each church needs all of the gifts of the Spirit to be operating to their highest level of efficiency and efficacy. What is the best gift? The one that is needed at the present time. The prophetic gift seems to activate or stimulate or encourage the other gifts. This has become more obvious to me over the years of ministry. For this reason alone, it is an important gift.

We are not meant to collect gifts of the Spirit in a display case. They are tools for the work of the Church, and the work of the Church is the work of Jesus in the world today.

The work of Jesus is often not very glamorous. *Minister* or *ministry* means servant or service. When people say, "I want to get into the ministry," they often do not understand this. They should be saying, "I want to become a servant." When people get "into ministry," they go and get themselves plugged into some ministry organization. Instead, they should be getting plugged into what the Master wants them to do. I guarantee that He will never instruct them to go out and minister all alone.

The recorded advancement of the New Testament Body of Christ—as clearly related in Acts and the Epistles—shows growth as organic: Life giving birth to New Life, whether one-on-one or in a larger gathering.

God's values honor each individual person as vital, yet as each person is giving and receiving, they are completing something more magnificent: The Bride of Christ.

God Wants the Whole Church to Be Prophetic

First Corinthians 14:1 gives us some practical advice: *"Pursue love, yet desire earnestly spiritual gifts, but especially that you may prophesy."* So the first thing that needs to happen is that you need to *desire*. You cannot just sit in a pew hoping that God will download revelation into you.

The other reason Paul wrote this is for the sake of the Church. Even when a person desires to become prophetic, that will not be enough if they do not also desire to love and serve their brothers and sisters with the gift of prophecy. You do not get a license to prophesy as if you are getting a driver's license. You do not get credentialed. You are supposed to lay down your life in service, listening to the One who is the greatest Servant of all and doing what He tells you to do.

You are supposed to narrow your focus to one purpose: edifying other people, building them up. The Word says it this way: *"Since you are zealous for spiritual gifts, let it be for the edification of the church that you seek to excel"* (1 Cor. 14:12 NKJV). You need people to prophesy to, and you need people to keep your head on straight. You also need to find people who need to be released into the prophetic gift, people to whom you can impart something from your prophetic supply.

God wants the whole Church to be prophetic, just as He wants the whole Church to be evangelistic and fervent in worship. Part of the prophet's job is to activate, stimulate, and release other Christians to be prophetic, biblically prophetic, which means that they will use their

prophetic gifts to cooperate with and enhance the operation of other spiritual gifts in other people.

In a very real way, as I have said already, the entire
Christian life is prophetic because its basis is an ongoing relationship with the living Lord, and that relationship involves communication back and forth. No question
about it, God wants the whole Church to be alive, serving
and loving as He directs.

What Does the Prophetic Church Look Like?

I believe that the Church as a whole should have a
high prophetic profile and that individual churches should
too, regardless of their denominational labels. "High prophetic profile" does not have to mean "weird."

It simply means that the Church is motivated by what
God says, which of course includes His written Word. (As
I indicated in the Introduction, a prophetic person "reads
the red." In fact, if you want to be certain that you are
delivering a prophetic word, simply reiterate the words of
Jesus as you find them in your Bible.) The church with
a high prophetic profile is a church that is moved by the
anointed words of God.

That kind of church does not have to be wild and loud,
with so many programs you need a channel-changer to
figure them out. A prophetic church may be big or small,
noisy or quiet. It may have a lot of programs or only a
few. The distinctive characteristic of a prophetic church
is that it listens to God before it does something. Will God
inspire special programs with clever names like Jogging
for Jesus, Karate for Christ, and the like? Maybe. Maybe
not. Will He rouse a group of people to fast and pray all
night? Will He equip and send teams of people to other
countries? How will you know what He's doing? For the
most part, you will know which things are God's ideas by

the fruit they bear. You will also know by the evidence of health in that particular body of believers.

So, what does a healthy prophetic church look like? While the specifics may vary, there will be certain indicators of health.

Here is an important one: I mentioned above that prophets focus on edifying other people. To *edify* means "to build up." A prophetic church will always build people up morally and spiritually. In other words, *a prophetic church is a place of edification.*

Such a church is dynamic, but not because of hype. It is dynamic because of love and light. When you are involved in a church that is a place of edification, you will feel built up morally and spiritually. You may come in too tired to worship, but something will change as a result of walking in the door. You will go home encouraged and strengthened because of the teaching and exhortation, the sense of purpose, the awareness of community.

Another feature is that *a prophetic church is a place of comfort.* People will always find security in an environment of intimacy with the Lord, and nothing cultivates that environment better than prophecy. Through prophets, God says, "I am with you. You are My people." You can hear it in the words of people, and you can see it in their faces.

Without a doubt, *a prophetic church is a visionary church.* It has direction. It is moving somewhere. As a body, the people are taking observable, realistic steps in a certain direction. They are not just going through the motions, and they are not imitating anybody else. They are on a journey together toward a particular destination.

A prophetic church is *not* like a flight simulator. Allow me to explain. Though it may surprise you, I still like flying. I have jumped out of airplanes even after the accident.

(Can you imagine that? You would think I would learn.) I just love thrills and action. And I know about flight simulators. A flight simulator could almost give me the same thrills because they are really sophisticated these days. They can give you simulated weather; they hit thunderstorms; they vibrate and shake; they lose altitude; they ice up—and they can "crash." But when you walk out of a flight simulator, you have not traveled anywhere. Some churches and ministries are a little bit like that, replete with special effects.

A prophetic church, however, is actually moving. It is going somewhere, and the people in it are eager to reach the goal. Unafraid, the leaders of a prophetic church are leading their people into their promised land. The prophetic destiny of a local assembly is both individual and corporate. Having and showing sincere love for one another means encouraging one another to fulfill His purposes for each life.

The leaders of a prophetic church understand that all of the gifts in the church need to cooperate. *A prophetic church is cooperative.* The various parts of the church will be in cooperation with each other, and they will be equipping each other. Their church identity will not be all about evangelism or all about Bible teaching— or all about prophecy. In fact, each of those gifts will be busy building up the others. In the past we have noticed a certain amount of tension between the prophets and the pastor/teachers, for instance. In a healthy prophetic church, even the strongest personalities will all be listening to the same Lord, and they will all be on the same page. I cannot tell you how much I have benefited as a prophet from sitting under good teaching. Note, I said, "sitting *under.*" I have surrendered my right to be right all the time about the revelations I get from God. I need other people to hold me accountable. It is good for me, and it is good for the church.

We are not holding a gift-competition. We are playing different instruments in the same symphony. We are in concert. The only one we are in competition with is the devil, who is trying to divide us and cause us to misunderstand each other.

We are imparting blessing and capabilities to each other. I am not a natural administrator, but in the past eight or ten years I have been around some good administrators, and I have learned to do some administration. I prefer to use my primary gifts, but in a pinch, I can administrate. I am more energized when I preach and pray and prophesy. An alligator is made for the swamp. Yet I can appreciate the uniqueness and diversity that God has created in the Body of Christ and the wonderful complementary nature that He has built into it.

United We Stand; Divided We Fall

When I was a skydiver, I wanted to hang around with other skydivers only. I idolized skydivers, and I felt that I was part of an elite cadre. But the Church of Jesus Christ is a motley crew. Most of us have nothing in common except Jesus. We differ from each other on so many levels. We rally together only because of the Lord. He calls us His Body on Earth, His family, His flock, His Bride—all of us put together. He loves us all, and He makes us able to love and appreciate one another.

Over the past decades, the Church has been through some ups and downs. Pastors have failed their people, and Christians have flailed at each other. Sometimes it has seemed as if the Church in America was wandering in the wilderness.

Yet God has been faithful, and now I believe we are rounding a corner. Along with a renewed emphasis on intimacy with Him, we are also hearing more about unity. This is not a fake unity, like a big stand-up cardboard picture of people with cutouts for their smiling faces. It is unity based on righteous character. God has something better for His Church than just coping—He wants us to reign.

Wherever you can have true unity with another Christian, with integrity, go for it. Do not abide division. Whatever you can do to grow in holiness and encourage others to grow in holiness, go for that, too. Holiness is not the same as religiosity. Holiness comes from God's grace. It develops from spending time in His presence, when your spirit and soul get imprinted with God.

With a united heart, God's people are seeking Him in prayer as never before. They are walking in communion and conversation with the Lord, returning to a deep personal relationship and a constant experience of His presence, but from a more mature perspective than before. The Body of Christ is hungering for more than an internal, personal blessing. People are longing for true revival. They are looking for more than a nice bonfire to warm their hands. They want to go up in flames for God.

A prophetic church encompasses all of these things. Discerning the difference between the voice of society around them and the voice of their Shepherd, they are going after the real meaning of belonging to Him. As Jesus said:

> *This is My commandment, that you love one another, just as I have loved you. Greater love has no one than this, that one lay down his life for his friends. You are My friends if you do what I command you* (John 15:12-14).

The Right Kind of Church

When I got out of the hospital and became part of a church, I did not know the first thing about what a healthy church should look like. The church I picked prided itself on being a "New Testament church," a "Bible-believing church."

This church worked hard to assemble the right kind of worship team and the right government, and we talked about cultivating the right fruits and gifts of the Spirit. Also, we wanted to make sure that everybody *knew* we were the right kind of church.

It was not a bad place at all. In fact we were highly influential and very committed. But the people did not fully grasp the idea that the Church (capital C, universal, which is made up of all the lowercased, local churches) belongs to Jesus. We thought we were doing the right things, combing the Bible for clues about what the church should be like. Honestly we had a slight eye disorder, tunnel vision!

In a prophetic church, you will not be able to find the evidence of rightness by evaluating the worship, the governmental structure, or the nice-looking, ideal personality types sitting in the pews. The testimony of a prophetic church matches Revelation 19:10, *"...the testimony of Jesus is the spirit of prophecy."*

The spirit of prophecy cultivates and unifies all of the other traits of a healthy church. In a healthy, prophetic church, Jesus is exalted, His Spirit moves freely, life-giving streams of God flow without impediment, Christ-likeness is an achievable goal, and all of the externals conform to His likeness. When people visit a healthy prophetic church, they meet Jesus.

The testimony of Jesus is the spirit of prophecy, and the testimony of whether a church is prophetic or not hinges on what the people *do* with what they hear from Jesus.

Jesus told His disciples a story about a man who had two sons (see Matt. 21:28-31). In modern-day vernacular the story would go something like this:

"Boys," the man said, "I want you to go out and work in the vineyard today." One of them said, "Dad, I'd rather play video games," and he stayed inside; but the other one said, "OK, I'm there," but he did not go to the vineyard after all. A little later, the first son changed his mind and decided to obey his father, but the one who had acted like he was going to obey never quite did it.

Jesus asked which son ended up doing the will of the father. Which one was like the right kind of church?

Prophecy—Personal or Corporate?

A prophetic church does not identify itself as such because it happens to have a famous prophet-pastor or a well-advertised "school of prophecy." A prophetic church may meet in somebody's living room, but it overflows with life. The life-flow of a prophetic church consists of the very words of the Lord of Life.

In such an environment, individual prophets do not stick out. Since all of the people are prophetic in a variety of ways, they fold themselves together into the fabric of the church, each one contributing something. They are not lone rangers; neither are they part of a faceless mass. They value each other's contributions because they all have the same goal—hearing and obeying their Lord. The life of the Spirit flows through the whole Body.

Much of the time, talking about prophecy involves talking about the mechanics and protocols of receiving personal "words." Prophetic individuals often say, "I just want to do what God wants me to do," but they get hung up on making decisions. Paralyzed with the enormity of the task, they do nothing.

On the other hand, some people get shipwrecked because they believe that they themselves must hear and interpret for themselves only. They spurn outside sources, except perhaps the ones that purport to teach them better techniques for hearing God. They can get a little weird.

John's first Epistle seems to endorse the solo approach to hearing God:

> *As for you, the anointing which you received from Him abides in you, and you have no need for anyone to teach you; but as His anointing teaches you about all things, and is true and is not a lie, and just as it has taught you, you abide in Him* (1 John 2:27).

This seems to be proof positive that we *are* all meant to be lone rangers. Who needs others? Just "abide in Him," and He will tell you everything you need to know, right?

But even the Lone Ranger had Tonto; they were a team. And if you want to abide in Him, you are going to have to abide in His Body, the Church. Before John made that statement, he made it clear that he was writing to the Body of believers, "little children," and "young men," and "fathers." Then he wrote about how you can distinguish the "antichrists," and he gives a simple test of who they are—they are the ones who have left the Church.

> *They went out from us, but they were not really of us; for if they had been of us, they would have remained with us; but they went out, so that it would be shown that they all are not of us* (1 John 2:19).

Now, that does not mean that every person who has ever left a church is an antichrist. It simply means that a person who claims to be a prophet, but who has removed himself from the fellowship of the corporate Body of Christ, should not be trusted blindly. He or she cannot expect to hear God accurately and consistently without the checks and balances of the rest of the Church Body.

The most common way that the Lord will speak to you and guide you is through His Church. Of course every person needs to have an individual relationship with Him, and that relationship should by definition be a prophetic one, but most commonly God is going to speak to you through prophetic teaching and preaching, through worship, through somebody else's ministry, and through circumstances.

Itinerant Prophets

Which brings me to the subject of itinerant prophets, in particular those individuals who do not stay rooted in a local body of believers, but who prefer to rove from one church to another carrying the word of the Lord in their backpacks with them. They are the ones who have chosen a lifestyle that precludes ongoing, ordinary relationships with fellow Christians.

Being part of a local body provides protection from deception in a very practical way. The great, mystical Body of Christ all across the globe and throughout the millennia boils down to individually planted local cells. In a local church, the people know each other. These people live in the same geographical region. They go to local places of employment and send their children to local schools and they go to each other's homes. They do not only attend weekly church meetings together; they come to know each other as human beings.

In the context of a local body, the judging of prophetic words, especially directive words, can be based on many factors, not the least of which is how committed the person is to the welfare of the intended recipients of the word. The prophet's character and track record will be common knowledge. Accountable to others in the church, he or she will not deliver "drive-by" words or commit "hit and run" prophecy.

What about people like my wife, Barbara, and me, prophetic people who have made a career of traveling away from home to minister? I think you will discover that most of the men and women who travel from one venue to another, preaching and prophesying at conferences and other events, are not isolated lone rangers. Everyone we know in similar ministries has both strong local and extra-local relationships, often also with specific accountability to peers. Some of them may have been dispatched by their home churches to minister to a broader audience. They spend significant portions of time with their spouses and families in their home churches, venturing out with their blessing and prayer covering.

Hands On in a Prophetic Church

A very precious older man of God named Lattie McDonough, who has been a father to our home church and to many individuals, including my wife and me, is a prophet. He puts it succinctly when he says, "Of all the ministries, the prophetic ministry needs to have hands on."

That is the truth. Prophets not only need to have their hands on the people to whom they minister, they need to have their hands in the dishwater and on the handle of the lawn mower. They need to be grounded in the reality of daily life, surrounded by committed, believing friends who can help them interpret what they hear from God. Being connected with the Body of Christ gives them a greater degree of stability and accuracy.

Abiding in the Lord means abiding in His flock.

All of the gifts that the Holy Spirit has given to the Church have been given to the Body and should be valued by the Body. A healthy prophetic church is a place where all of the people are prophetic because all of the people seek to be directed by the Lord in everything they do.

A Sending Prayer

Father, thank You that the prophetic ministry is as simple as being born again, listening for Your voice, and becoming part of the Body of Christ. Thank You that it is not some far-out, mystical, hard-to-get assignment that forces people to go live in caves in the desert.

Thank You that in fact our individual prophetic ministry can and should take place in the context of Your prophetic Church, in local churches. We want to be planted in the Body of Christ, and we want to grow and flourish there. Bless our local churches with loving, wise leadership and healthy, prophetic direction. Bless them with Your life-giving Spirit. Bless them with a spirit of edification, comfort, vision, cooperation, and true unity in Your Son.

When people visit our local church, may they meet Jesus! Amen.

Chapter 3

Revelation and Faith

The greatest adventures can be found in the realm of the Holy Spirit. Speaking as someone who likes to travel as fast as possible and who loves taking risks, that is a significant statement to make. With all that God has done for me to restore my body so that I can play with my kids, go swimming, ride a motorcycle, jump out of airplanes, ski so fast that sparks come off my skis—I still would rather have five seconds under the anointing of the Holy Spirit, who sends the best adventures of all.

Whether or not you have an adventurous personality type as I do, God made all of the different personality types, and He knows how to bring you into the fullness of an experience of His presence. He wants to do that for you because *people*, collectively and individually, are just very important to Him.

Not only does He love us human beings enough to have sent His Son Jesus to redeem us, He also has set things up so that He needs to use people to accomplish His will. He even sent His Son as a man to be our intermediary.

After that, He sent His Spirit directly to each individual. You can see that God has invested Himself in the people who comprise His Church, equipping it to move out in great things—by faith.

By the faith of His people, God manifests Himself in the world. All of the things that happen when the realm of His Spirit touches the Earth—the healings, the miracles, the demonstrations of power, the prophecy—are activated by faith. And that faith is highly personal, relational, one-on-One. It is as if God is holding hands with each person.

Where does this relational, connectional faith come from? It comes from the One who sends His Spirit of revelation to us so that we have a clearer idea of what He wants us to do. Revelation from God releases faith in God. Our own insight and wisdom will never be enough. Paul put it this way:

> And when I came to you, brethren, I did not come with superiority of speech or of wisdom, proclaiming to you the testimony of God. For I determined to know nothing among you except Jesus Christ, and Him crucified. I was with you in weakness and in fear and in much trembling, and my message and my preaching were not in persuasive words of wisdom, but in demonstration of the Spirit and of power, so that your faith would not rest on the wisdom of men, but on the power of God (1 Corinthians 2:1-5).

Like Paul, you probably figured out a long time ago that your human abilities were going to be no match for the requirements of life with God. Through the circumstances of your life, the Lord made sure that you would come to the end of your own resources. Be glad that He does that! I know it seems counterintuitive, but falling to your knees in weakness and fear and much trembling is always the first step toward faith. Crying out to the Lord opens the windows of Heaven. God will always reveal Himself to you in some way. His prophetic revelation will always reinstate your faith and spark new faith. Your faith will become an avenue to joy-filled strength and victorious adventures.

Rising From Unbelief

Do you remember the Bible story about the desperate father who sought healing for his epileptic son? Clearly, the man had reached the end of his own resources, as well as the resources of his family and friends. Even the disciples, who were Jesus' own companions, had not been able to help him.

Then Jesus Himself showed up (in other words, this desperate dad received a visitation from God, which is the best kind of revelation to receive), and Jesus inquired of the man about his son. The father burst out—

> *"...if You can do anything, take pity on us and help us!" And Jesus said to him, "'If You can?' All things are possible to him who believes." Immediately the boy's father cried out and said, "I do believe; help my unbelief"* (Mark 9:22-24).

Each of us can identify with that desperate father because we, too, have a degree of faith. But we need a fresh revelation of the Son of God in order to have *enough* faith for whatever we are facing at the moment. Just as Jesus healed and delivered that boy, based on his father's heartfelt plea (note—the father himself did not have to be Superman), so does Jesus come through for you and me, based only on our plea for more ability to trust Him.

We trust Him because He has proven that He cares. We trust Him because He has revealed Himself to us and because He has proven His faithfulness time after time. Over time we learn reliance on the Spirit of revelation for the release of more faith. Life becomes a faith-adventure as God gives us ever-increasing faith.

A well-known leader and church-planter during the Jesus movement told me that he was raised in a church where he recalls people saying, "God told me this," "God told me that," about everything. He says he knew it could not possibly be all God speaking; instead it had to be a bunch of people talking to themselves. So he decided to just stick to the written Word.

However, in the late 1980s, he got into the prayer movement, and he started hearing the voice of the Lord for himself. He had spent a great portion of his life in ministry neglecting and even repudiating the prophetic ministry, even to the point of allowing a stronghold of unbelief to block it. Now he found out that people really could hear from God and realized that knowing that could have been very valuable all those years. This is a common cause of unbelief. There are reasons why people shut down and block the prophetic. But God's love never fails. In this time of strong emphasis on re-turning to our first love, we are rediscovering the voice of God.

Without Faith, Nothing Happens

Faith is nothing unless it is exercised. I do not think you could say it even exists unless it is being actively used. Somebody like you or me has to exercise it. Faith is a forward-looking *action.*

You can have faith in many things besides God— faith in your abilities, faith in your spouse or your pastor, faith in the food you eat, faith that when you go through an intersection, other drivers will not run a red light.

Every kind of faith starts with a degree of prior knowledge about something, a comprehension, some level of understanding.

Revelation is just a more elegant word for what you need before you can have faith in something. To be able to exercise the kind of faith that I am talking about in this chapter requires an extra boost of understanding about the Kingdom of God. Something more will have to be revealed to you.

To move in faith, you will need revelations—plural— from God. You will need timely revelations. To position yourself to receive them, you will need to have an ongoing relationship with Him through His Spirit. Then He can speak to you easily. He can show you the things you need to know, and you can therefore operate in faith, following Him in a surefooted way. Every time He reveals Himself to you, you get to know Him a little better, and your faith grows a little more.

Paul prayed for the believers in Ephesus to receive the spirit of wisdom and revelation so that they might know God better:

> *I keep asking that the God of our Lord Jesus Christ, the glorious Father, may give you the Spirit of wisdom and revelation, so that you may know Him better. I pray also that the eyes of your heart may be enlightened in order that you may know the hope to which He has called you, the riches of His glorious inheritance in the saints, and His incomparably great power for us who believe...* (Ephesians 1:17-19 NIV).

He told the Romans, *"Faith comes by hearing, and hearing by the word of God"* (Rom. 10:17 NKJV), and that without faith nothing happens. The writer of the letter to the Hebrews wrote, *"Without faith it is impossible to* *please Him, for he who comes to God must believe that He is and that He is a **rewarder** of those who seek Him"* (Heb. 11:6).

God is the giver, and we are the receivers. But we cannot receive a thing from Him without faith, which we get by hearing *by the word of God* (see Rom. 10:17). *"Hearing by the word of God"* is the same as revelation. Personal revelation has power. It alters our perception and our worldview. It transforms our minds, emotions, and wills. For example, look what happened to Nathanael.

"I Saw You Under the Fig Tree"

Nathanael went from scoffing unbelief to absolute faith because Jesus told him, "I saw you under a fig tree," when He was definitely not close enough to the fig tree to have seen Nathanael with His natural eyes. Jesus had a revelation about Nathanael being an honest man, and when He told Nathanael about also seeing him under the fig tree, Nathanael received immediate faith about Jesus:

> *Philip found Nathanael and said to him, "We have found Him of whom Moses in the Law and also the Prophets wrote—Jesus of Nazareth, the son of Joseph."*
>
> *Nathanael said to him, "Can any good thing come out of Nazareth?"*
>
> *Philip said to him, "Come and see."*
>
> *Jesus saw Nathanael coming to Him, and said of him, "Behold, an Israelite indeed, in whom there is no deceit!"*
>
> *Nathanael said to Him, "How do You know me?" Jesus answered and said to him, "Before Philip*

called you, when you were under the fig tree, I
saw you."

Nathanael answered Him, "Rabbi, You are the
Son of God; You are the King of Israel."

Jesus answered and said to him, "Because I said
to you that I saw you under the fig tree, do you
believe? You will see greater things than these."
And He said to him, "Truly, truly, I say to you,
you will see the heavens opened and the angels
of God ascending and descending on the Son of
Man" (John 1:45-51).

The revelation released Nathanael's faith. That is the wonderful way it works. At first Nathanael had no faith whatsoever. His response was not faith-filled. Then because of Jesus' revelation, the needle on his faith meter went all the way from unbelief to belief.

Jesus uses Nathanael's response as a jumping-off point, telling him that this is only the beginning. Seeing someone under a fig tree is a word of knowledge, a brief snapshot of revelation. But Jesus promises that before the end of his life, Nathanael will *"see the heavens opened and the angels of God ascending and descending on the Son of Man."* In other words, Nathanael can expect to receive much greater revelations in the future. And so should we!

Jesus' statement refers back to what happened to Jacob when he had the vision of angels ascending and descending on the ladder to Heaven (see Gen. 28:10-18). Every Jew knew that story, and they knew that it had occurred at Bethel. The name Bethel means "the place of God." The revelation of God happens in the place of God, in God's presence.

Faith Is Relational

Many people see faith as a means of procuring answers to prayers. They miss the fact that the faith is a built-in part of their relationship with God.

As you relate to God, He reveals Himself to you and you get to know Him better. The things you may have heard or read *about* Him suddenly gel and you "get it." Faith is, therefore, both relational and revelational.

Faith is a key to the Kingdom of God, and the spirit of revelation releases it. Without revelation we flounder around. With revelation (sometimes on a very simple level—the fig tree revelation was not deep theology) we stand up and start walking—in clear-eyed, clear-hearted faith. Revelation sparks faith and sets it ablaze. Revelation changes us from being muddled and earthbound to being focused and Heaven-sent.

Simon Peter got a definite revelation when he identified Jesus as *"the Christ, the Son of the living God"* (Matt. 16:16). Jesus took the opportunity to change the course of Peter's life. Immediately, He re-named him *Peter*, which means "rock," a much stronger name than his original name, Simon, which means "hearing," adding that He intended to build His Church on Peter's rock-like faith (see Matt. 16:18). Immediately also, Jesus promised, *"And I will give you the keys of the kingdom of heaven, and whatever you bind on earth will be bound in heaven, and whatever you loose on earth will be loosed in heaven"* (Matt. 16:19 NKJV).

Jesus was not iffy about building His Church. All in one sentence, He was building a boulder of faith into the very foundation of His Church, and He was handing over the keys of Heaven not only to Peter, but to every disciple who would name the name of Jesus.

How do we use the keys of Heaven? Well, think about the function of a key. With the keys you carry in your pocket, you can open (or shut) something or start (or stop) something, right? If you put your car key into the ignition, your car roars to life and you drive away. Arriving at your destination, you take the key out of the ignition and put it back into your pocket, and your car stays in the same place until you want to drive it again. It is the same with the keys of the Kingdom of Heaven. When you use your faith, you take action in both the heavenly realm and on the earthly plane. Ignited by faith, things happen that could not happen any other way. Without the keys, nothing happens.

Faith is as much of a hard and firm reality as your car keys are. Even though you cannot see it with your eyes or feel it with your fingers, faith is as solid as a rock. Faith is far more than five little letters, F-A-I-T-H, that spell an overused English word. I have "faith" in my doctor, "faith" in the cab driver, "faith" in the sturdiness of my chair to hold me without collapsing.... Yet from reading the Bible, I find out that *"faith is the substance of things hoped for, the evidence of things not seen"* (Heb. 11:1 NKJV). Faith is invisible, but it is solid.

Faith translates hope into actuality. In a world of uncertainty, we may not know what is going to happen in the next five years, but we know, by faith, that God will be with us. We may not be able to rely on so-called facts or the information we can gather, but we can rely on the God who has revealed Himself in Jesus Christ and who continues to reveal Himself day after day to us.

He calls Himself the author and finisher of our faith (see Heb. 12:2). God is not hiding elusively in the shadows. He is poised for action. He is Life itself. He is manifesting Himself to us all the time through revelation.

Do you desire to have more revelation and, therefore, more faith? Or have you always assumed that you would just have to resign yourself to wait for the Author to finish your faith on His eternal timetable? Is it possible for you to position yourself for more revelation and its resulting download of faith? These are not trick questions.

Revelation Imparts Hope

Before you can trust in the present tense with strong faith, you need some future-tense hope. Another translation of Hebrews 11:1 goes like this: *"Faith is being sure of what we hope for and certain of what we do not see"* (NIV). Your faith is not the same as your hoped-for objective. It is the means of obtaining it. But if you are not hoping for something, you will not even bother to put the key of faith into the ignition. You will not have a destination in mind, and you will not want to budge.

An amazing example of hope can clearly be seen in one of the stories of the ministry of John the Baptist, recorded in Luke's Gospel: *"Now while the people were in a state of expectation and all were wondering in their hearts about John, as to whether he was the Christ...."* (Luke 3:15). Hope is active expectation, not passive resolution. (Some people think, "Well, we will just see what happens. We'll see if God does something, 'if it be Thy will.'")

The Bible refers to, *"Christ in you, the **hope** of glory"* (Col. 1:27b). When God's Spirit of revelation shows you your options, you get a little more excited. Now you have *hope*, and it is far better than some kind of nebulous optimism. Hope will help you keep your focus.

Your hope is an expectation or a desire for the future, and it has to do with waiting. Faith has to do with *how* you wait. Look at the connection: *"We through the*

Spirit, by faith, are waiting for the hope of righteousness"
(Gal. 5:5).

After my accident, but before I was swept up into
the heavenly realm by the Spirit, I was in a hopeless
condition. No one was giving me a whisper of hope for
recovery. Medical experts had given up on me, and my
body was so devastated that there was no way I could
have mustered anything like hope or faith by myself.
However, in the glorious presence of God, I received the
hope that no one on Earth could give me. I came back
knowing that I would be eternally cared for. I came back
carrying seeds of faith for an untold number of future
challenges and difficulties.

Without a revelation of the Lord Jesus Christ, we can
have no such hope. The Spirit of God is with us at every
juncture of our lives. He is Emmanuel, God *with* us. He
never fails, even when the journey seems long and dark.

No Darkness Is Too Deep

Invariably, the Lord is going to put you into situations that will call for more faith than you have on hand.
Whenever that happens, He wants you to ask Him for
another revelation about His resources and for more faith
to unlock them.

The story of Jesus and the disciples in the boat on
the stormy sea is a perfect illustration of this:

*Now when Jesus saw a crowd around Him, He
gave orders to depart to the other side of the
sea....*

*When He got into the boat, His disciples followed
Him. And behold, there arose a great storm on the
sea, so that the boat was being covered with the*

waves; but Jesus Himself was asleep. And they came to Him and woke Him, saying, "Save us, Lord; we are perishing!"

He said to them, "Why are you afraid, you men of little faith?" Then He got up and rebuked the winds and the sea, and it became perfectly calm.

The men were amazed, and said, "What kind of a man is this, that even the winds and the sea obey Him?" (Matthew 8:18, 23-27; see also Luke 8:22-25)

This was no little sea squall. The disciples, who were not lacking in nautical experience (many of them had been professional fishermen before they started following Jesus), were terrified. They thought they were going to drown. Nothing from their considerable experience on the water suggested otherwise. And yet Jesus actually rebuked their lack of faith—of course increasing their faith in the process.

This was something new for them. It was beyond all of their previous experience. From this experience, they learned that when Jesus says that you are going to the other side, you are going to make it to the other side. They also learned that this does not guarantee a storm-free passage.

A major storm may be brewing, and you may end up right in the middle of it. But while your boat is being tossed around on stormy waves and you are hanging on for dear life, you *can* have faith. You may not be able to quell the storm at all, but you can cry out to Him for help, and the Lord will use the stormy seas to ramp up your faith even while your knuckles are still white from hanging on so tightly. If you call on Him (even if He seems to be sleeping), you will get the help you need, and you will be less likely to fall prey to terror next time the same kind of storm comes around.

Barriers to Revelation and Faith

Believe me, I know about storms, and I know how many things can get in the way of your revelation and faith. Besides false assumptions, questions, and doubts, you can be buffeted by storms of hurt and offense. Like the disciples on the boat, you can look no farther than the nose on your face, evaluating your fearful circumstances only by means of your own human ability to think things through and your previous experience.

Of course you end up worrying instead of praying, preoccupied and consumed by your problems. You cannot figure out what to do, and you second-guess yourself mercilessly: "Did I make a bad decision? Did I pray and fast enough? Is the church going to come through? Did I say enough? Did I say too much? Why is this happening?"

Let me tell you a little secret—when you find yourself in a low spot faith-wise, *do not* ask yourself too many questions. When you are in the middle of something, do not brood about it, because your over-thinking will attract darkness. Your ruminations will get you into more trouble. Some of the voices that you hear will be dark voices. While you are so busy looking inward, you will find it harder to look upward to the Lord.

Looking inward is the same as relying on your flesh, and you already know that the strength and resources of your human flesh will not suffice. Unhappily, with your mind set on your own resources (or maybe on someone else's human resources), you will usually have to get into much deeper quagmire before you will cry out to God alone.

Paul wrote a firm letter to the people of the church in Corinth, which was a Spirit-filled church *"not lacking in any gift, awaiting eagerly the revelation of our Lord Jesus Christ"* (1 Cor. 1:7). In spite of their spiritual credentials, they were slipping into the all-too-human tendency to trust leaders more than they trusted in Jesus. Paul chastised them:

> *Now I plead with you, brethren, by the name of our Lord Jesus Christ, that you all speak the same thing, and that there be no divisions among you, but that you be perfectly joined together in the same mind and in the same judgment. For it has been declared to me concerning you, my brethren, by those of Chloe's household, that there are contentions among you. Now I say this, that each of you says, "I am of Paul," or "I am of Apollos," or "I am of Cephas," or "I am of Christ." Is Christ divided? Was Paul crucified for you? Or were you baptized in the name of Paul?* (1 Corinthians 1:10-13 NKJV)

Paul wanted the Corinthian believers to be able to mature past their childish divisions so that they could receive some deeper revelation. He wanted the best for them. He wanted them to grow up. He did not want them to get so far in their life as a church only to founder in the end.

Sometimes you can get right to the edge of doing what God has called you to do only to fall short, failing to persevere past the most daunting part of the difficulty or settling for a solution that does not involve faith. That is what happened to Peter when, in his unbridled zeal, he led the other disciples in vowing to Jesus, "I am ready to die for You! Even though others may fall away, I will never deny You" (see Matt. 26:33-35). Even when He heard it, Jesus knew better. He knew that Peter's faith would fail and that every one of them would desert Him. It took a series of miracles to bring them back.

When Jesus sought Peter out after His resurrection, He gave him three affirmations of His love to counter Peter's three adamant denials (see John 21:15-19). Peter was so broken. He was totally aware of his own human limitations, his failure, his tendency toward reacting impulsively instead of acting in faith. Jesus gave him a second chance, and Peter was restored. (When you get a revelation of pure, undiluted Jesus, He can fix up your wounds so that you are stronger than you were before.)

Emerging From Darkness

In this season of severe storms in the world and in the Church, I believe that the Lord is shaking off the junk that His people are hanging onto. He is showing us how broken we are. He is smoking out the phoniness and making sure that those who identify themselves as Christians will begin holding more tightly to His Son, Jesus Christ. He is bringing to our attention the fact that the Church that once had the name of being alive has died to its innocence because of hurt, offense, human failure, and the weakness of the leaders. He is making us realize how thirsty we have become as we've been trusting in our own broken cisterns:

> *For My people have committed two evils: They have forsaken Me, the fountain of living waters, to hew for themselves cisterns, broken cisterns that can hold no water* (Jeremiah 2:13).

He wants us to learn to deplore our limitations—so that we will be desperate enough to turn and receive and believe and become all that He wanted us to be when He created us.

At the same time, He is pouring out the spirit of revelation so that we can see in the dark, by faith. He is restoring the years that the evil one has consumed. Most of all, He is restoring us to Himself.

Unlimited Access

So, to recap: Faith is primarily a relational thing, and it comes by revelation. The Greek word for "revelation" in the passage that I quoted at the beginning of the chapter (see Eph. 1:17) is *apokalupsis*. It means disclosure, manifestation, appearing, coming, illumination. It comes from a root word that means "to take the cover off."

Sometimes the revelation takes awhile to penetrate. How many times have you heard something with your ears, but your heart was not involved? Sometimes you have heard a teaching or sung a song or read a Scripture a hundred times without anything special happening. Then on the hundred-and-first time—boom!—suddenly the truth becomes personalized to you. It speaks to your heart. You have a brand-new sense of living reality. It becomes the living word because it comes alive to you. Suddenly the cover comes off; there is illumination—and confidence.

No longer do you have to try hard to figure something out. No longer are you limited to your intellectual comprehension. When that revelation comes to you, suddenly faith rises up and everything changes. With the spirit of revelation active, you *know* God has spoken—to *you*. You really do not care what anybody else thinks because you know in your spirit that God has spoken to you. The Holy Spirit has communicated with your spirit, bearing witness with your human spirit that God is intimately involved with your circumstances. The evidence is the tremendous jolt of faith that surges through you.

Here is an example from our personal experience. A number of years ago we were given a free trip to Israel. It had been our desire for some time to go on this tour, and it seemed especially timely because of certain circumstances in our lives. We were there less than one hour when my wife Barbara stepped off the tour bus and shattered her ankle in multiple places. Suddenly we were in a hospital in Tel Aviv and the X-ray showed that she needed surgery. I went outside and prayed, and amidst the swirl of confusion I heard the Lord say, "Take the best care of your wife that you can." So I went back in and said, "Barbara, I'm taking you home to America." She was so disappointed; she would have been willing to worship the Lord at the Feast of Tabernacles while sitting in a wheelchair.

Our friend and tour guide preserved the finances for the next trip. About 18 months went by, but we just could not fit it in. Finally Barbara just said, "I really feel I'm supposed to go; I'll just travel with my friend." So she got the wheels turning, and she was all set to leave when just two days before departure, I checked on her travel plans. Someone had made an administrative mistake at the airline and there were no seats available—disaster! I hassled with the airlines for about a day and a half (and I happen to be a pretty adamant telephone hassler), but finally Barbara said, "Mickey, I know it's God's will that I should go, but this is too stressful for you. I'm going to lay it down." Meanwhile, in my mind, I was considering whether God might be resisting the trip because of the danger of going to Israel at that time.

Some time passed, and Barbara remembered a prophetic word she had received in Nashville, Tennessee. She dug through her purse and found a cassette tape with that recorded prophecy on it. It talked about her broken ankle and her burden for Israel and her heart to intercede for that nation and how God would bless her when she was in the Land. Instantly, she shot up on her feet and threw her fist up in the air: "That's it! I'm getting on that plane, and I'm going to Israel!" She packed her suitcase and jumped in the car to go out to buy a few remaining items for the trip. When I heard the door slam, I thought, "Wow, I hope she's not going to be disappointed again." Then I started my role as Mr. Mom. As I was loading the dishwasher I heard the Spirit of God say, "I really like that about your wife," and I said, "I really like that about her too."

Before she came back, the phone rang and Mr. TWA, some high-ranking official, told me that there was *now a seat on the airplane.* Her upsurge of faith got her a seat on that airplane when it was not possible!

This is not a super-spiritual type of thing that happens only to a few people. Every believer should be able to relate to this. Even the moment of your salvation was a moment of revelation plus faith. Suddenly you could *see.* Without hesitation you could say yes to whatever God wanted you to do. Ever after, you would be able to manage your life differently.

You would have to cultivate your relationship with God, but that is the same as cultivating the spirit of revelation, with the result of being able to enjoy an ever-increasing ability to walk in faith.

How can you explain it? The supreme God who commands the affairs of the universe wants to give you, personally, communion with Him as often as you choose to relate to Him. *He wants to relate to you.* He wants to make it possible for you to grow in your relational faith.

He has work for you to do, and He takes great pleasure in showing you the way. *"For we are His workmanship, created in Christ Jesus for good works, which God prepared beforehand so that we would walk in them"* (Eph. 2:10).

Through His Spirit, God is revealing the way, and His Spirit searches all things:

> *...Just as it is written, "Things which eye has not seen and ear has not heard, and which have not entered the heart of man, all that God has prepared for those who love Him."*
>
> *For to us God revealed them through the Spirit; for the Spirit searches all things, even the depths of God* (1 Corinthians 2:9-10).

The Spirit is speaking a language of revelation to the spirit of any person who will receive, and His revelation is like fertilizer for growing faith.

A Sending Prayer

> Father, we want to live in Your power. We want You to rouse us away from the weakness of our flesh and make us alert in our spirits to Your Spirit. We want to bypass distractions and focus on You.
>
> Surprise us with Your Word. Shape us with it. Reveal Yourself to us through both Your written Word and the prophetic words that are all around us. Give us eyes to see, ears to hear, and hearts to hold the revelation that You want to give us. Transform us more and more into Your image, Jesus. Amen.

Chapter 4
Maturing in Prophetic Ministry

You and I are in process. Year after year, we are changing and maturing into the people God wants us to be. Much of our maturing process happens by default as we grow through our life experiences and try to understand them. Every now and then we even dare to give God permission to mature us a little more.

Our goal: Christlikeness. When I think about maturing in prophetic ministry, which is the subject of this chapter, naturally I think of growing more skilled in practical ways and becoming better at discerning and delivering the word of the Lord. But it is so much more than that. Prophetic maturing will take care of itself as long as we are allowing the Holy Spirit to mature us into the image of Christ Jesus.

We need to flip our assumptions. Maturing in prophetic ministry is secondary to becoming Christlike people who happen to have prophetic gifts. We need to become Christlike people with prophetic lives.

What Does It Mean to Be "Mature"?

I always feel like a schoolboy. Lately I have begun to realize that feeling like a perpetual learner is actually one proof that I am maturing. For that reason, I hope I never "arrive" until the day I go home to be with Jesus.

I have heard of the Lord touching men who were in their 80s, after they had retired from long, successful ministries, and all of a sudden they were like dynamos for the people around them. I hope He will touch me like that. I do not want to crystallize or ossify or get static or be locked into a box. I always want to be open to discovering more avenues for knowing the Lord and for expressing His love to others.

I have had the privilege of working with some of the most gifted people on the Earth today, and I have seen some amazing things. But along the way, I have met no experts, only other learners and followers of Jesus. There is always more to learn because the mind of Christ is as vast as the universe. To be mature simply means that we have gotten more hints into His grandeur than we used to have. The evidence of maturity is a liberated, humble love for God and the things of God.

The reason God has planted gifts in each of us is so that they can grow in our spirits like fruit-bearing trees beside the streams of living water. He wants to nourish and mature our spirits, souls, and bodies so that we can help to nourish and mature others. He does not want us to disparage the prophetic gifts or any other gifts in the name of false humility or because we think it is selfish to concentrate on such things. On the contrary, He invites us to ask for more.

How much more will the Father give to those who ask Him? (See Luke 11:13.) He wants us to seek to increase the activity of the Holy Spirit in our lives, which includes His activity through our gifts.

Specifically for the prophetic gifts, what does it mean to be mature? Here are a few aspects of prophetic maturity:

- Mature prophets know that the Lord did it. "It was great. I was part of it, but I am just a little helper."

- Mature prophets *receive* impartation and training—always. They never outgrow the need for mentoring, teamwork, biblical study, and literal impartation of spiritual anointing.

- Mature prophets *give* impartation and training—generously. They release others into greater ministries, looking for ways to push people ahead of themselves.

- Mature prophets are humble servants. They celebrate the advancing excellence of others, without jealousy, even if their gifts are "running hot." In that hour Jesus *"rejoiced in the Spirit and said, 'I thank You, Father, Lord of Heaven and earth, that You have hidden these things from the wise and prudent and revealed them to babes. Even so, Father, for so it seemed good in Your sight'"* (Luke 10:21 NKJV).

- Mature prophets collaborate with others; they are servants. Even a superstar prophet like Elisha learned prophetic maturity by pouring water on the hands of his master, Elijah, and he did not mind being known as his servant.

- Mature prophets value the baby steps of faith, and they practice walking in faith. They know that walking step-by-step in faith will increase their sensitivity to hearing God's voice.

- Mature prophets do not get as excited as immature prophets do. When sensational prophetic headlines go public (positive or negative), a mature prophet takes it in stride. He or she is all too aware of the human factors involved in the gift of prophecy.

Mature prophetic people know that the best part of using the prophetic gift is seeing someone else benefit. Throughout their lives, they place a high, high value on edification for the common good (see 1 Cor. 14:12). That is what they get excited about. They love to see someone else benefit or get blessed. Because they hold edification and building others up so high, mature prophets do not much care who gets the credit. They cooperate with other gift ministries and anticipate the fact that God will use a wide variety of people and circumstances to accomplish His will.

"Cut the Baby in Half"

The foretelling, predictive aspect of the prophetic ministry is its most obvious characteristic, but a more foundational aspect of the prophetic function goes far beyond mere events, circumstances, or dates. The well-rounded prophetic gift is a tool in the ministry of spiritual interpretation, a gift of wisdom. Like the sons of Issachar (see 1 Chron. 12:32), prophets are people who can determine the signs of the times and can discern what to do about them.

Unlike some self-proclaimed prophets who perpetually foretell catastrophic judgment and other bad news, seasoned prophets are not gloom-and-doom people. They speak *into* bad news situations, proclaiming the good news of God and interpreting the spiritual climate of a church, an individual, or even a nation. Prophets with a proven track record possess knowledge about which path to take for advancement and improvement, and they communicate that information in a way that people can receive.

There are so many no-win situations in Christian churches, most of which involve leadership. The tension of conflict is extreme, and people try to come up with solutions that will work. They try to negotiate deals, find scapegoats, and cut their losses. But it seems as if whatever people do hurts somebody else.

I do not want to be trite, but "what would Jesus do" in a conflict? When people tried to trap Jesus, He would get a word of wisdom. So should prophets, who are by definition becoming more Christlike. I am trying to say it in as many ways as I can: Prophetic maturity is largely wisdom. Mature prophets are wise people, and they get their wisdom from God.

Solomon's famous demonstration of wisdom involved a real live baby, squirming and squalling. Two women claimed to be the child's mother, and they wanted King Solomon to judge between them (see 1 Kings 3:16-28). It was a contentious situation, and I am sure the members of Solomon's court were holding their collective breath to see what he would say. He considered the scene before him. "Well," he said, "just get a sword and cut the baby in half and give half to one mother and half to the other." The real mother proved herself by wanting to protect the child, even if he had to be given to her rival, whereas the deceitful mother revealed herself to be more concerned with her rights than with the welfare of the baby she was claiming. Solomon gave the baby to his true mother, and the conflict was ended.

This kind of wisdom from God is essentially prophetic because the wise word of the Lord comes into the situation and along with it comes peace. When Jesus was challenged on the subject of paying taxes, His answer made it impossible for the Pharisees to trap Him: *"Render to Caesar the things that are Caesar's, and to God the things that are God's"* (Matt. 22:21; Mark 12:17; Luke 20:25).

When the people brought Him the woman who had been caught in adultery, He bent down and wrote in the dirt. I think He was waiting for the Spirit to show Him what to do. I think that after He stalled for time, the Holy Spirit told Him what to say: *"He who is without sin among you, let him be the first to throw a stone at her"* (John 8:7). Then after her accusers had all dropped the stones from their hands and slunk off, I believe that the Lord Jesus could discern that she had a repentant heart, so He could tell her what to do: *"Woman, where are they? Did no one condemn you?... I do not condemn you, either. Go. From now on sin no more"* (John 8:10-11).

The wisdom of God always wins. You can ask the best counselors, read the best how-to books, attend the best seminars, and go on the best experience and advice you can find, but without the wisdom from above, your solutions will not last very long.

Not Rocket Science

That being said, I want to add a quick disclaimer. You do *not* need a revelation from God about everything. Sometimes the only wisdom you need to walk in is common sense.

For example, take a godly principle such as fasting. Should you fast or not? Just read the red. The Lord Jesus Himself said, "*When* you fast..." (see Matt. 6:16-17), not "*If* you fast."

Well, then, how about financial giving? Should you give when you are strapped for money? Can you just hold off for a while until you get more money? Anyway, isn't tithing and giving too "religious"?

For my part, I am just going to keep giving to the work of the Kingdom. Concerning giving, there are tithes, offerings, and alms. It does not take a rocket scientist to figure this out. A very close friend said to me recently, "I don't even know what tithing is anymore. I just give at every offering." This was said during a time of extreme suffering and risk at just being alive and keeping the work functioning. I do not need a revelation about giving, and I do not need a complicated algorithm to figure out where my money should go.

No Peter Pans

Peter Pan always said that he never wanted to grow up. I guess he thought he would be able to keep on having fun if he stayed immature. I may be advocating simplicity and common sense (and fun, too!), but I am not advocating immaturity on any level. We are in a cosmic spiritual battle, after all. God has equipped His Church with the gifts—apostle, prophet, evangelist, pastor, teacher, and more—that are necessary for health and victory (see Eph. 4:11).

I know a pastor in California who preferred to keep out of spiritual warfare. He thought it was over-hyped. And besides, it can get so messy. Then the Lord spoke to him prophetically and said, "I am going to teach you about spiritual warfare."

At first he welcomed the idea because he thought God was going to teach him mainly how to avoid "three- and four-hour sessions with people foaming at the mouth and barfing in my office." He said, "God is going to just teach me how to cast demons out right away. That will be great. I will really be equipped."

You know what God did? He painted a big bull's-eye on that guy's shirt, and every demon that wasn't busy doing anything went down to his house and began to hang around. He encountered spiritual warfare on such a level that he was driven down onto his face. Then the Lord taught him about intercession and instructed him about the protection of people who are praying for you. He also taught him the wisdom of not spouting off your mouth every time you think you have a revelation, as Peter did when the Lord said, *"The devil has demanded permission to sift you like wheat"* (Luke 22:31).

The pastor began to get a little wisdom and maturity about good and evil. He matured in knowledge, discernment, and patience. No longer did he expect to graduate instantly from spiritual warfare class with his certification and a ticket to easy ministry.

Like an immature kid, he had wanted everything *now*. But maturity means learning how to wait. Not only does a mature prophet know how to stall for time as Jesus did when He wrote in the dirt, a mature prophet has also learned so much patience that he or she can never deliver a word at all if the circumstances are not right.

One time I had a personal word for a sister in my church, and it sure felt like a "right now" word. When it came, it was "hot." Then the Lord said, "Wait a minute." I paused for a moment, and the stirring lifted.

Eight months passed! One Sunday morning, again the prophetic unction came on me, and I prophesied the exact word to her; and when I opened my mouth to speak, a whole bunch more words came with it. She was enormously built up, and she could confirm everything. She told me that the word was a lot more appropriate right then than it would have been earlier because the circumstances of her life had served as a time of preparation.

For me this was a lesson in *finer tuning*. To bring a fruit-bearing word of God, you need revelation and interpretation, plus fine-tuned application that is even more than just obeying a "wait a minute" that turns into an eight-month minute. But why had it felt so much like a "now" word if I was supposed to hold it for eight months? Maybe it was because the word came from the eternal heart of God. In His "time," which is outside of our time plane, every word is a "now" word, isn't it? It takes a certain level of mature patience and a willingness to wait long enough to get instructions about the application for a word, the timing, and anything else the Lord may want to give you.

Barbara and I first had three boys and then we had a baby girl. At the moment Elizabeth was born the Lord spoke to me, "This will be your last child." Then, *whoosh,* a powerful impartation of the Spirit. Overwhelmed by the force of God I was crying, praying, worshiping, and I didn't even know what was going on, except it was glorious! Twenty years later at the altar just after Elizabeth and Bryan said their vows, what had been brewing for all this time was declared to them. It was a stunning, beautiful, life experience that I will cherish all my days.

Maturity brings charity. A prophet who is growing will be developing patience with him- or herself as well as with fellow prophets who may not be as experienced. You will have plenty of opportunities to grow in this one. When you deliver (or hear someone else deliver) a word that reveals an "attitude" or that seems to be ill-timed or that employs a poor choice of words, what are you going to do? If you are maturing as a prophet, you will understand the growth process, and you will "cut some slack" to yourself and others. You will understand how delivery and timing can be a bit off, and you will make allowance for it. You will be able to tell if God wants you to say anything or make changes. If you cannot decide how to handle the situation, you can look for another prophet with more experience and ask him or her for advice.

Growing in Discernment

The wisdom of a mature prophet is closely related to the gift of discernment. Pray for discernment—you need it all the time.

As I noted above, prophets who are growing in discernment are learning how to accept others just the way they are, not trying to *adjust* everybody all the time, but rather simply loving them. At the same time, prophets should be open to receiving adjustment themselves. They should be teachable and "adjustable."

As it turns out, most people with a prophetic gift tend to be very "black and white" people. They find it difficult to give people latitude. They ignore others who do not receive exactly the same revelation at exactly the same time in exactly the same way. Sometimes they can seem like know-it-alls, as if they think that everybody else is just backslidden or brain dead. (I am exaggerating, but just a little.)

A mature prophetic person can walk into a situation and say, "This is a house of God. Therefore, God is probably doing something good in all of these people. I will not be overly critical, and I will look for the best way to build these people up."

Even Jesus had to mature and grow in wisdom and discernment (see Luke 2:52). Think about it. As He grew into manhood, undoubtedly He could discern everything around Him. I am sure He could not help seeing and knowing things. But He showed wisdom and obedience to His Father by holding back until He was 30 years old, and even then He spoke up only when it was judicious to do so.

I am sure that you have read Amos 3:7, which tells us, *"Surely the Sovereign Lord does nothing without revealing His plan to His servants the prophets"* (NIV). God does not do anything on the Earth without also revealing it secretly somehow to some prophet somewhere, even if it is hundreds of years before it happens.

When we hear a statement like that, we often feel a little dubious about it. This is perhaps because so many of those prophets held back the revelations God had given them—to their credit. We may not know about them because they were never broadcast or published. Quite likely they either did not know what to do with the information or they asked God about it and He never gave them the green light. It is something to think about.

A lot of times people think they have discernment along with a prophetic gift, but they just use their prophetic insights as an excuse to beat people up verbally. According to Francis Frangipane, all you really need is one eye and a carnal imagination in order to do that. That is not discernment; it is judging people after the flesh. Just because one person's clothes are funny or another person is in a bad mood is no reason to prophesy that they have an evil spirit or that they are steeped in sin.

It should go without saying that if we are modeling our prophetic lives after Jesus and allowing His Spirit to speak through us, we will not use our prophetic gifts to condemn others or to drive them into a corner with no way out. We can use our gift for conviction (maybe), but not for condemnation.

Let It Settle

As a protection for the people around us as well as ourselves, we must learn to judge and discern our own words. Most of us fail to do this to the extent that we should. After reading and listening to all kinds of advice about judging prophecy, we need to remember that judgment and discernment are much more than simply deciding whether a word is from God or not, whether it is "good" or "bad" or "just my imagination" or "of the devil."

Discernment literally means the act of sorting something out to see what is there. Picture yourself sifting through a pile of something so that you can distinguish what the pile is composed of. Using your senses such as eyesight, smell, touch, and especially your spiritual sensitivity, you sort through everything in the pile, including motives, the current environment, and much more. This can take awhile.

The Bible says, *"We know in part and we prophesy in part"* (1 Cor. 13:9), and we prove it every day. Inevitably we do an imperfect job of receiving and conveying God's words to others. I would say that as much as 50 percent of a lot of the prophecy we hear in public is "add-on." The core of the word may be right on, but out of the whole pile of verbiage, only about 50 percent will pass all of the discernment tests. A word can start out from God, wander into the flesh, and end up back in God. Another word could start out in the flesh and then suddenly get into the flow of God.

But as long as both the givers and the receivers of the words are growing in their discernment and humility, that is all right. Most people do not realize that it is OK to wait a little. Instead, they just "let 'er fly." If they would only "let it settle" awhile, they could consider a word more carefully with the help of the Holy Spirit. If it is a corporate word, before they even deliver it, they could share it with the pastoral leadership and then just let it settle—in other words, do nothing.

One way to let a word settle is to record it or type it out. Then you can listen to it or re-read it, pray over it, ask God what it means, and watch for the places where your spirit has a "check" as well as the places where your spirit bears witness that something is truly from God. This will help especially with volatile words, those words that generate an immediate emotional reaction in the recipient or recipients—so much of a reaction that they may miss the rest of the word.

As a word settles out, all of the givers and receivers can learn a little bit more about hearing God. Everybody will learn that while words from God may contain some new information or some fresh impartation, most of a word will simply confirm what they already know in God. It will reinforce or confirm the truth. In other words, it will be true to the written Word, and it will ring true to the Spirit of the living Word who dwells in the hearts of believers.

Wandering Stars

Vital to the discernment process is having somebody who knows about the life of the particular prophet. A prophecy delivered by a "lone ranger" prophet lacks this safeguard. Lone rangers are not attached to anybody. Even if they deliver the word of the Lord, I do not want to listen to it because I do not know if I can trust the source.

The Bible talks about people who are like wandering stars or clouds without water:

> *For certain persons have crept in unnoticed, those who were long beforehand marked out for this condemnation, ungodly persons who turn the grace of our God into licentiousness and deny our only Master and Lord, Jesus Christ.... These are the men who are hidden reefs in your love feasts when they feast with you without fear, caring for themselves; clouds without water, carried along by winds; autumn trees without fruit, doubly dead, uprooted; wild waves of the sea, casting up their own shame like foam; wandering stars, for whom the black darkness has been reserved forever.... These are grumblers, finding fault, following after their own lusts; they speak arrogantly,*

*flattering people for the sake of gaining an advan-
tage* (Jude 4,12-13,16).

A wandering star has no fixed relationship. People
who are like wandering stars have no fixed relationships
with other Christians. Nobody is guiding them. Even if
they start out as truly anointed, they get off track when
they stop being accountable to peers who can speak into
their lives. Often, the greater a person's gifting is, the
greater the danger of self-deception. Soon people start
thinking they are superstars when really they are merely
a flash in the pan.

The truth is that each one of us is only a sheep. We
need to be with the rest of the flock. When I am with the
other sheep, I am nobody special. The others know all of
my little bumps and warts, and yet they love me. They
care for me, they will help me, and they will make sure I
do not get off track.

A person who is all alone may be very gifted, but out
of insecurity or some other issue, they will end up getting
blindsided all the time.

Nobody Understands Me

Sometimes people with prophetic gifts feel that they
are not being heard. "Nobody understands me. Nobody
listens to me. I have the prophetic anointing, and I get
prophetic revelation, but nobody pays attention to me."

Tongue in cheek, I say that instead of being God's
man of power for the hour, this kind of person may be
only God's man of paste and flour. (Might as well open a
wallpapering business....) "See, you really do not understand," they reply. "Prophets get rejected. The reason I am
getting rejected is because I have the anointing." Is that
so? Most of the time these people are an annoyance.

Anyone who starts to slip into the "nobody understands me" syndrome needs a reality check. The Lord does understand us, and He loves us even when we start thinking too highly of ourselves. He is interested in maturing us so that we can get past our whining. We happen to be in pretty good company at our pity party—I see Elijah over there in the corner.

Remember what happened to him? First, as we read in First Kings 18, he confronted the prophets of Baal on Mount Carmel. It was a tremendous prophetic act. Then Queen Jezebel threatened his life and he ran. Hiding in a cave, he was saying to himself, "Nobody understands me. Everybody rejects me. Out of all the prophets, I am the only one left" (see 1 Kings 19). He was so depressed that he wanted to die. That is pretty extreme, and yet it seems to be a common prophetic flaw. Moses, Jonah, and others fell into it too. When Elijah fell into the "nobody understands me" syndrome, God made him face it. He wanted him to become more mature.

God does not want us to be self-centered or to isolate ourselves. He wants us to get past being prophetic crybabies. He has plans for us that may involve tough situations. We need to be willing to face them.

It Is OK Not to Know Everything

Many times prophetic people put a lot of pressure on themselves because they think that a prophet has to be all-knowing. Then when they do not understand something, they start making things up so that they will keep sounding "spiritual."

It is OK not to know what everything means. In fact, *often* we will not comprehend the meaning of a word or a vision. Sometimes it will be because of our inexperience, and at other times it will be because the word encompasses too much for our puny abilities of comprehension. It is OK not to know everything—and it is a sign of maturity to be able to say so.

Daniel was one of the premier prophets in the Bible, and yet he could barely understand the revelations he received. In chapter 8 of the Book of Daniel, the angel Gabriel interpreted for Daniel one of his visions, and then he told him:

> *"The vision of the evenings and mornings that has been given you is true, but seal up the vision, for it concerns the distant future."*
>
> *I, Daniel, was exhausted and lay ill for several days. Then I got up and went about the king's business. I was appalled by the vision; it was beyond understanding* (Daniel 8:26-27 NIV).

Even with the help of an archangel, the vision was incomprehensible to Daniel, and he was a basket case for a while. But Daniel was mature enough to accept the fact that he would never be able to understand the vision and then to rally and begin to serve in his normal capacity again. He did not worry about the fact that the vision was beyond his understanding and that he would not live long enough to see what happened.

Next time you have a prophetic experience, rest in the knowledge that God is in control and not you. Do not stop learning and growing in your wisdom about interpreting what you see and hear, but do not put too much pressure on yourself either. Like Daniel, you can simply say, "I may not understand a fraction of this thing, which may make me look kind of ignorant, but I am OK with that. I am just going to take care of my normal responsibilities and keep trusting God."

Don't Take Yourself Too Seriously

Very early in my ministry, I had a dream that has affected me to this day. At the time, we were living in a farmhouse, and in the dream, I was standing on our front porch. Across the street was a passenger bus that was stuck in the mud. I went over there, and I could see that it was full of frightened passengers who wanted to get out. I couldn't hear them, but they were banging on the windows, and I could see their mouths moving, "Get us out!"

At the time, I used to watch Pat Robertson on television on the *700 Club*. In the dream, there he was, looking at the bus, dressed in a three-piece suit. Then he looked at me in my work boots, jeans, and flannel shirt. He looked back and forth several times, and I expected that he was going to do something.

I pointed my finger at the people and I said, "In Jesus' name...." Even before the phrase was completed, the windows and doors of the bus popped open and the people were set free. I was shocked and I exclaimed, "Bless God!"

Immediately, I was in a tow truck speeding down the road *backward*. It took all of my effort to stretch my foot out to depress the brake pedal. As I pushed with all my might, I was awake and sitting up in my bed.

Then the Lord spoke to me and He said, "When you start releasing people with My power, don't take yourself too seriously. You can start to go backward."

This was a loving explanation and a warning, and it is a good example of how God can teach us, prepare us, and warn us through dreams. Prophetic revelation is an asset, but in no way is it a human attribute. I would be shortsighted to take myself too seriously as a prophet, even when I see miraculous results. At the same time, I need to regard the Lord very seriously. He is the source of the power.

Perfect Love Casts Out Fear

Our best safeguard against immaturity, which includes feelings of insecurity, fear, pride, and rejection, is always going to be our personal relationship with God. Remember—the prophetic life is all about that all-important relationship between a person and God. He is the One with perfect love. He *is* love (see 1 John 4:8).

His perfect love will cast out any fear. *"There is no fear in love; but perfect love casts out fear...and the one who fears is not perfected in love"* (1 John 4:18). Notice that *love* is the key ingredient to victory over fear. Not faith. Not hope. Not perseverance. Elijah had more faith than anyone we will ever meet, enough faith to taunt and challenge the bloodthirsty prophets of Baal, to stack the deck against himself, and then to literally call down fire from Heaven. He had gigantic faith. But right afterward what do we see? There is the mighty man of faith fleeing from the threats of a woman who's wearing too much makeup! His perfect faith could not prevail over his fear of punishment and death. But the perfect love of his God could.

Prayer connects us with the perfect love of the Father. In our praying, we admit that there is a Supreme Power in the universe that is incomprehensibly big and yet personal, clearly He is Lord of all, and we respond to the invitation to engage in a conversation with Him. Prophetic people must be people of prayer. Prayer is a lifestyle. Prayer is weakness. We remind ourselves that we need Him on a daily basis. Free to be honest, we find our full security in Him. Once in a while, He passes on some information to us, and we call that "prophecy."

The whole time we become more and more aware that we are merely a vessel. Maturing as believers (and therefore, as prophetic people), we will find it easier all the time to recognize the difference between the hand of God and our own hands. God is like a surgeon, and we are like the medical gloves He puts on when He wants to carry out an operation. He uses His sharp instruments with skill, and when His task has been completed, He pulls off the gloves and throws them away. We are important to the process, but we are only the vessels for His Spirit. We are only the gloves. The hand of God is what moves us.

No matter how wise, proven with awesome experience, stay a learner/novice and you keep on maturing.

A Sending Prayer

Lord of love, we humble ourselves under Your mighty hand. We ask You to make us able to clothe ourselves with true humility. Our prayer is an act of humility, and so is our worship. We are utterly dependent upon You. Without Your Spirit, we cannot be good servants, let alone people who are able to share Your word with others. We know that humility will attract Your grace, and grace is what we need in order to become all that You intend us to be.

You love us so much that You sent Your only Son, Jesus, to purchase us from the slavery of rejection and sin. We are much more confident in Your commitment to us than we are in our commitment to You. We still fail. We get discouraged, confused, and fearful. We suffer from our immaturity. And yet we know that if we keep coming to You daily, surrendering our rights and our pride, You will have Your way with us.

We want to love You and bless You in every way. We desire to grow up and to become as mature as possible. We want to grow in our ability to use prophetic resources, but most of all we want to grow in our love for You. May it happen because of Your love. Amen.

Chapter 5

Dreams and Visions

The key to our relationship with God is communication. The Spirit of God has always wanted to communicate and commune with the spirits of the people who belong to Him. He wants to hear from us, and He wants to respond to us. He wants us to hear from Him, and He wants us to respond to Him. Communication is a two-way street. As we all know if we think about it, communication takes place on many levels. Words, spoken or written, are only part of it.

The apostle Paul prayed for the men and women in the church at Ephesus. One of the parts of the prayer that is recorded at the beginning of his letter to the church concerns getting to know God better:

> [I pray] *that the God of our Lord Jesus Christ, the Father of glory, may give to you a spirit of wisdom and of revelation in the knowledge of Him. I pray that the eyes of your heart may be enlightened, so that you will know what is the hope of*

His calling, what are the riches of the glory of His inheritance in the saints, and what is the surpassing greatness of His power toward us who believe... (Ephesians 1:17-19).

One of the ways that He pours out His Spirit of wisdom and revelation on us to enlighten the "eyes" of our hearts is through visual means—through dreams and visions. In fact much of the language of the Spirit seems to be expressed in this way. While we may communicate with God mostly in words and gestures of our hearts, He seems to prefer to communicate with us in pictures.

To hold up our end of the communication, our part is to learn the special language of the Spirit. We need to become good listeners and good "seers." It is something like adding video to our audio feed—and it has been happening for hundreds of years. In the time of Moses, God reiterated the way He had set it up:

[God] *said, "Hear now My words: If there is a prophet among you, I, the Lord, shall make Myself known to him in a vision I shall speak with him in a dream"* (Numbers 12:6).

The difference now is that the "prophet among you" is *you!*

Book of Acts Today

When I was in the hospital after the skydiving accident, the only times I prayed were when I was scared (which was often) or when I did not understand something. I knew nothing about the Church and nothing about how to cultivate a relationship with God. But God was good enough to help me out, many times through dreams and visions. He made sure that I was being changed in my spirit even as I was being rehabilitated in my body.

Although I did not yet know much about God's promises in the Bible, I was part of their fulfillment. I found
out later about the words of the prophet Joel that Peter
had used in his sermon at the beginning of the Book of
Acts, preaching to the crowd of people in the street:

> *This* [the remarkable manifestations of spiritual
> power that had caused the crowd to gather] *is
> what was spoken of through the prophet Joel:
> "And it shall be in the last days," God says, "that
> I will pour forth of My Spirit on all mankind; and
> your sons and your daughters shall prophesy,
> and your young men shall see visions, and your
> old men shall dream dreams; even on my bond-
> slaves, both men and women, I will in those days
> pour forth of My Spirit and they shall prophesy"*
> (Acts 2:16-18).

I did not know it until later, but the visions and
dreams God was giving me in the hospital were ground-
ing me in Him so that I could communicate with Him
and also so that I could tell others about Him. I had been
drafted into the army of God. His Spirit was being poured
out on this messed-up scrap of humanity named Mickey
Robinson just as freely as He had poured Himself out on
the day of Pentecost.

God was communicating with me directly. To hear
Him, no longer would I need to rely on a priest or a board-
certified prophet with a name like Isaiah or Jeremiah.
The prophetic had been made personal, and the flow of
His Spirit would continue.

How many others are in on this secret? How many
others can encounter the Lord in dreams and visions?
The answer, since the day of Pentecost, is *everyone*. Encounter is available to anyone who has responded to the
voice of the Shepherd and who is learning to follow Him

(see John 10:27). Jesus explained it this way: *"The Helper, the Holy Spirit, whom the Father will send in My name, He will teach you all things, and bring to your remembrance all that I said to you"* (John 14:26).

God longs to lead and guide us. He wants us to have an intimate relationship with Him even while we are still walking on this Earth with all its distractions. He has some pretty impressive ways of getting our attention, and they include dreams and visions.

History-Changers

The Bible is filled with references to dreams and visions—220 references, to be exact. Some of them seem to have been almost incidental, but most of them were not. In fact sometimes the future of an entire nation was contingent on someone's response to a revelation in a dream or a vision. Sometimes it was even more important than that; the future of generations of the human race depended on one individual hearing the voice of God while he was sleeping.

Think of Joseph's dreams about ruling over his brothers (see Gen. 37:5-9). One thing led to another, and years later he was serving as prime minister of Egypt when his brothers showed up—as beggars. They had not known that they were playing into the hand of God when they sold their younger brother into slavery. But because of the fulfillment of those prophetic dreams, their family would not starve to death after all. Through dreams Joseph saved not only himself and his family, but also the entire nation of Israel. His dream had further consequences. Centuries later another one of the sons of Israel, Moses, would lead them back to their own land by following God's explicit instructions, which were verbal, but also visual.

Much later, a different Joseph had a dream in which an angel told him to take Mary as his wife even though she had become pregnant and he knew he was not the father (see Matt. 1:20). After her baby had been born, he had another dream in which an angel warned him to take the baby Jesus and His mother out of the danger of Herod's slaughter. He obeyed, and he took them to Egypt where they stayed until Herod died (see Matt. 2:13).

Do you see how these dreams shaped history? And I am not even taking the time to describe all the ways the dreams fit with other prophetic words. Through the Holy Spirit God identifies and reemphasizes His will through dreams and visions. The people who receive the words are not schooled or trained in the art of dream interpretation. Sometimes they do not appreciate the interruption. (Think of both Cornelius' and Peter's visions in Acts 10.) But the Holy Spirit is the instigator who gives dreams and visions liberally, making the prophetic word visual and, therefore, more personal—and even more accessible to everyday folk like you and me.

Tuning In

Each of us is a spirit with a functioning soul that lives in a body. Although our bodies grow old and die, our spirits and souls are immortal. The "soulish" part of us includes our free will, our emotions, our memories, our deductive reasoning, and our mind. It operates independent of God:

> "For My thoughts are not your thoughts, nor are your ways My ways," declares the Lord. "For as the heavens are higher than the earth, so are My ways higher than your ways and My thoughts than your thoughts" (Isaiah 55:8-9).

However, God makes it possible for us to tune in to His mind and His will through our spirits. God's Spirit speaks to our spirits, and our spirits bear witness to it so that our minds can understand what He is saying. This is called revelation. It does not work the other way around; you cannot figure God out. *"Now we have received, not the spirit of the world, but the Spirit who is from God, that we might know the things that have been freely given to us by God"* (1 Cor. 2:12 NKJV).

Jesus, quoting the Book of Deuteronomy, said, *"It is written: 'Man does not live on bread alone, but on every word that comes from the mouth of God'"* (Matt. 4:4 NIV). Our spirits thrive when they are well-nourished with the words of God, and that does not mean only the words written down between the covers of the Bible, but also the words that His Spirit speaks to our spirits and the pictures He shows to our spiritual eyes.

I keep repeating the importance of relationship and communication. The revelatory realm is a major part of God's communication system, and prophetic people are like telecommunication receivers.

When prophetic people receive pictures, they are "seers" because they are seeing the word. When you dream a dream sent by God or see a vision (even a fleeting one), your "receiver" is being exercised in the seer capacity. You are discerning spiritual things with your spirit, and you are learning to be more alert.

Especially in the Western world, the whole process involves a steep learning curve. We are very accustomed to relating to the world around us only in terms of what we can fathom with our five natural senses or figure out with our brains. We assume that if we cannot smell, touch, see, hear, or taste something, that it is not real. Little do we know that an invisible spiritual realm is often closer to us than the chair we just sat down on.

People have spiritual lives whether they are aware of them or not, and they are affected by spiritual forces whether they believe in them or not. Even atheists have spirits, and therefore, they have spiritual lives. It is much better for us if we embrace the spiritual life that God brings to us. Jesus said, *"My kingdom is not of this world.... My kingdom is not of this realm"* (John 18:36).

Dreams in the Night

Research indicates that all of us dream, whether or not we remember it, and that we have as many as six dreams a night. Most of them are highly symbolic, often in extreme ways.

Dreams can be literal and symbolic at the same time. For example, a dream may portray something that has already happened or that is going to happen, while at the same time it could contain a symbolic teaching about forgiveness or love or caution. The dreamer may grasp one aspect of the dream right away and only understand the other aspect later. Or, of course, the person who had the dream may never remember or be able to interpret any of it.

The understanding of prophecy and dreams and visions is always very subjective. This fact does not invalidate them, but it does mean that different people will come up with different "takes" on things. Any one person can be influenced by previous experiences, relationships, emotions, or circumstances. For this reason, especially when a dream seems to carry a heavy message, it is important to subject it to thorough scrutiny from several sources including the written Word and a circle of trustworthy people who are close to the person who had the dream. One dream or dreamer cannot be considered greater or better than another; they are simply different. Yet we can find protection by getting outside input. *"Where there is*

no guidance the people fall, but in abundance of counsel-
ors there is victory" (Prov. 11:14).

Over the years, I have had many, many dreams and
so has my wife. Sometimes I get one half and she gets the
other half. Through these dreams, we have been warned,
guided, and taught. We have received confirmation and
information.

Once we had a situation in our church, and I had a
dream about it. There was this lady in our church who
was very gifted, but who was causing no end of trouble.
For years she had been undermining the leaders and cre-
ating havoc. Nobody knew what to do.

In my dream, I was in the back seat of a police car,
with two policemen in front, one driving and the other in
the passenger seat. Suddenly, the driver changed lanes
and started driving toward oncoming traffic. We were
moving really fast, switching lanes and going through red
lights. I had a sense of both authority and of potential
danger. After driving along like this, we stopped in front
of an average city block. I looked out the window. There
was a person on the street attacking another person with
a gun.

I yelled out something like, "Hey, don't!..." and all
of a sudden the attacker started coming toward the police car, pointing the gun at me. My window was open,
and I was trying to lean back out of the way. The attacker turned out to be this lady from church, and she
was pointing her gun right in the window. I was trying
to kick it away with my foot and wrestle it away from
her. Finally I got it, and I shot her with it. As she was
falling to the ground—blood everywhere—suddenly she
turned into my young son, Jack, but before I realized
that, I finished her off with another shot. Only now
it was my own son lying there in all the blood, dead.
"Oh my God! I just killed my own kid!" And one of the

policemen said to me, "You didn't have to do that." I woke up shaking.

Now you might think that was only a nightmare and that I should have ignored it. But I felt it was some kind of a warning from God. I felt that God was warning me that we should be very careful how we handled this woman because she was a child of God and that, even though she was attacking the leadership of the church to the point of trying to kill it, we should not "kill" her. Any of us would have liked to have taken her head off, publicly disgraced her, or disciplined her somehow so that she would either straighten up or get out of the church. But God was saying, "Be careful. Wait."

The interpretation of a dream is so important. I could have gone off worrying about harming my son somehow, but he was only a symbol in the dream.

I know about a man who misinterpreted a dream and his misinterpretation could have caused a lot of problems for himself and other people. He thought the dream applied to his whole church, and he thought they were supposed to declare a 40-day, church-wide fast, after which revival would break out. He took his dream to one of the leaders of his large church.

Wisely, the leader asked him more about the dream. The man said, "In my dream there was a clean and empty plate and there was silverware next to it, and an empty glass. Then I saw a calendar, one of those calendars with 'Monday, Tuesday, Wednesday' written at the top of each page, and the pages started flipping past until about 40 days went by. When I woke up I knew that the Lord was saying that the plate was clean and we shouldn't eat anything for 40 days and then revival would come."

The leader said, "Let me ask you a couple of questions. First, how are things going for you?"

The man answered, "Pretty good—and I really believe that when we do this we're going to get what we've been praying for...."

The leader interrupted, "And how is your prayer life?"

"Well," the man said, "It's all right. It's been better. I started working second shift. I've been working this extra job, and I haven't really been able to get to church or meetings, you know."

"How is your study in the Word?" the leader asked. "How has that been going?"

"Well, it's like, you know, I...well, come to think of it, I've heard some good preaching, but I haven't been reading as I normally do because I have been working so much."

"How long has this been going on?"

"Well, I took this new job a little over a month ago."

The leader paused. "Do you think," he said, "that maybe your dream means that you yourself have not been getting fed for that period of time?"

Bingo. "Oh wow. Thanks."

So instead of standing up in a church of 2,000 people and giving a directive word about the Lord showing him that all the men, women, children, dogs, and cats in the church must commit to a 40-day fast, which would have really messed people up and which would have destroyed his credibility, he went home and figured out how to get back on track with prayer and Bible study.

That dream was a true revelation. But it did not mean what he thought it did at first.

Dream Interpretation

To interpret dreams, people need to first be able to remember them. Dream recall can improve with a little practice. Besides getting plenty of sleep, vitamin supplements such as vitamin B_6 can help.

As an overview, here are some principles of dream interpretation.[1]

Decide that dreams reveal God's counsel. *"I will bless the Lord who has counseled me; indeed, my mind instructs me in the night"* (Ps. 16:7). A person who retains doubts about the value of dreams will not make much progress at interpreting them.

Study biblical dreams. Someone who reads through the story about Joseph's dreams or others can better appreciate the value that God puts on communication through dreams. Study biblical symbolism. See if you can figure out what nonbiblical symbols mean in your own dream life.

Ask God in prayer to speak through dreams. When people are asleep their bodies are slowed down, but their spirits are active, and God can engage them. God wants to be asked to speak through dreams. He says, *"Call to Me and I will answer you, and I will tell you great and mighty things, which you do not know"* (Jer. 33:3).

Record dreams immediately upon awakening. Everyone forgets dreams, even with the firmest of intentions to remember them. To help, some people keep a pencil and paper next to their beds. Others keep an audio recording device handy.

Keep an eye on the small details. You can have a long dream with people you know in it and a dramatic chase scene, and you could notice a hammer over in the corner. Later on, you could find out that the whole dream was hanging on that hammer.

Try to awaken naturally. Alarm clocks often shatter dream recall.

Do not make major directional changes without advice. Before selling the house and car and clothes and running off to the mission field, people should find a trusted spiritual counselor to whom to submit dreams that seem directive.

However, do act on dreams. Do not become passive. Do not assume that dreams mean nothing. Seek an interpretation. Hold the dream up to the objective standard of Scripture, away from the influence of emotion and personal prejudice. Then hold it alongside subjective opinions to see if the meaning emerges.

Do not pose as a dream-interpretation expert. Self-proclaimed experts are usually not trustworthy. Learning the language of the Spirit concerning dreams is a lifelong process and a spiritual gift.

Do not "live off" dreams. People who dwell too much on their dreams soon begin to live in La-La land. Dreams are wonderfully symbolic, but they are not meant to become an alternate universe.

Consider going to a spiritual counselor. People who are having spiritual problems as well as vivid dreams might benefit from an outside perspective.

Be patient. Sometimes God will give a dream, but the interpretation does not come for months or even years. Dreams about Armageddon may not be fulfilled immediately!

Visions

Visions are like "waking dreams" and pieces of dreams that a person sees when awake instead of asleep. (Conversely, dreams are "night visions.")

Often people dismiss the things they see as too insignificant to be considered visions, and yet they are. Very, very often a vision is what people call an "impression," something that people sort of see and sort of don't see. It can be brief, a snapshot of an image perceived with the inner eye or the retina of the mind. Many times it is symbolic. Sometimes it comes along with a word of knowledge.

When I am ministering to somebody, sometimes I see a little picture flash by, and I will comprehend the meaning of it. As I pursue it, as with a sense of a prophetic word, and begin to describe it or "talk around" it, a flow of meaning begins to come from the image.

People talk about "open visions." In my understanding, this is when a person can see with their physical eyes something superimposed on the natural arena. This seems to be fairly rare—although it is increasingly becoming more evident.

Even more rare is a vision received in a trance state. In these cases, the person is taken right out of the natural realm. Peter "fell into a trance" when he went up on the roof of the house that belonged to his host, Simon the tanner (see Acts 10). For a space of time, he was not aware of the roof or the sky or the smells and sounds around him. Three times, he saw a vision of a sheet being let down from Heaven, filled with all sorts of animals that were unclean according to Jewish law. A voice told him to "kill and eat," which was abhorrent to him. Then downstairs some Gentiles arrived from Cornelius' house to invite him to come tell them about God. If Peter had not had such a strong vision to convince him that God was overruling what he has always thought were His own laws, he would never have entered the "unclean" house of a Gentile.

Even though open visions and trances can seem a little weird to Westernized people, they are not much different from dreams. Extreme symbolism is the rule, not the exception. Our best insurance against deception is to stay very, very close to the Lord.

One time I was in bed asleep, and I was having a dream. Then I woke up from the dream, and I must have gone into a trance. I felt as if the bed was sitting still but the rest of the room was spinning around me in a blur, going a hundred times faster than a merry-go-round. I felt like Dorothy in the house being lifted by the tornado in *The Wizard of Oz.* I knew I was going somewhere. And in my lap was a huge book with golden letters and gold edges on the pages. I should have looked a little closer at the book, but I was so overwhelmed by the power of the experience that I shook it off. Instantly, I went back to normal and was just sitting in my bed. To this day, I do not know how I could have handled it any differently. It was an awe-inspiring blast of power. Perhaps the Word in my lap was being deeply imprinted in me and God gave me a "peek" while it was happening.

Most of the time visions are fleeting. A person can miss them. I believe that the ability to pick up more in the Spirit can be enhanced by prayer and worship. When people say, "I see" something, most of the time, they are not having an open vision, and certainly they are not in a trance. They have simply glimpsed an illustration of something that is coming from the heart of God. God is speaking His word using visionary language, and many times one simple vision will result in a flow of revelation in a person's life.

As with any form of a prophetic message, we should ask God what to do with a vision. We cannot assume that we should share about it on the spot. Too often, other people will not understand, or they may become offended or fearful. By staying in close touch with God all the time, we will grow in Christlike character and cultivate the fruit of the Spirit, which will increase our ability to handle visions with integrity, love, and patience.

A Visionary Life

We can generate what I call a "visionary life" in our spirits, tearing down walls and opening ourselves up to new experiences in the Spirit. Ideally we want the Holy Spirit to work through our human spirits to affect our souls (our minds and emotions). We want our imaginations to play back the things of Heaven, not the stresses of our daily life.

To help with this process, we can start by recording our dreams and visions and sharing them with people in authority over us, trustworthy people who have spiritual influence in our lives. We can ask for counsel and help with interpretation. And we can ask for help in applying them.

Believe it or not, about one-third of the Bible is directly or indirectly related to a response to a dream or a vision. For example, consider Paul's "Macedonian call":

> *A vision appeared to Paul in the night: a man of Macedonia was standing and appealing to him, and saying, "Come over to Macedonia and help us." When he had seen the vision, immediately we sought to go into Macedonia, concluding that God had called us to preach the gospel to them* (Acts 16:9-10).

Paul was already traveling and preaching, but God sent instructions to him in a dream to go to a different region. He obeyed, and many people were affected by that vision as the Kingdom of God expanded into a brand-new part of the civilized world.

In that same spirit (and in the same Holy Spirit), may we pay attention to every communication that comes from God and continue to grow in our ability to understand God's wild and wonderful language.

A Sending Prayer

Holy Spirit, we look to You expectantly. Speak to us through dreams and visions—and help us understand this special kind of communication. Keep us humble, but always alert to Your messages, day and night. We want to handle Your word with integrity, patience, and dependability, even when it comes to us in the form of fleeting pictures and subtle symbolism. Most of all, we want to keep growing closer to You, our spirits to Your Spirit. May dreams and visions increase our closeness with You. You are the Lord of our lives. Amen.

Endnote

1. No single chapter or book can cover the entire subject of dream interpretation. Recommended resources to help you understand how to interpret dreams include books by the following authors, listed here in alphabetical order: James Goll, Jane Hamon, John Paul Jackson, Morton Kelsey, Ira Milligan, Herman Riffel, and Mark Virkler. There are reliable resources that are biblically sound, yet birthed from ecstatic encounters.

Chapter 6
You May All Prophesy

John the Baptist never had an identity crisis. I believe his parents must have told him often, "We were not able to have any children, and we felt bad about it, and we prayed, and an angel appeared and said, 'You are going to have a special child.'" From his youngest years, John knew he was set apart and different, and he knew why he had been born. Years later when people came to him and asked him, "Are you the Christ?" he could assure them that he was not. "Are you the prophet?" No, again. "Well, who are you?"

"I am the voice of one crying in the wilderness" (see Matt. 3:3; Mark 1:3; Luke 3:4; John 1:23). The purpose of his life was to be the one who would preach repentance to prepare the way for the Lord who was coming. His job was to get people ready to respond to the Lord. John the Baptist knew he was the one Isaiah had talked about, and he also knew that he was not worthy to untie the sandals of this One who was coming.

We know that John the Baptist was a mighty man because Jesus said that of the men born of women, there was none greater than John (see Matt. 11:11; Luke 7:28). But Jesus also said that the least in the Kingdom is greater than John. That puts some responsibility on you and me. What does that mean about us? It means that our potential to be strong in the Spirit is greater than John's anointing. That is hard to believe. But on the other hand, we do realize that we have the Spirit of Christ Jesus dwelling inside us.

A Quickened Word

We are living in a season when the gifts of the Spirit are being restored, and we need to know how to grow up into maturity. We do not want to throw out the baby with the bathwater and stop desiring spiritual gifts, especially the gift of prophecy, but we do not want to mishandle the gifts out of ignorance, either. There are whole church movements that have outlawed prophecy because immature people have abused the gift.

If we want to know the fullness of prophetic reality, as I have been saying repeatedly, that reality is most fully evident in the life of Jesus Christ, both past and present. He is the living Word, and He dwells in our hearts (see John 1). He is the ultimate revelation. We do not merely learn *about* Him by reading the written Word; we have His pulsating presence within us, a quickened Word of revelation and love, and we need to learn how to appropriate it by grace. When the Lord by His Spirit quickens the Word to us, that is when the Word of God becomes prophetic.

Each one of us, regardless of our relative maturity, should be seeking to prophesy. The strongest argument in favor of that statement comes from the apostle Paul, who urged the members of the church at Corinth to *"desire earnestly spiritual gifts, but especially that you may prophesy*" (1 Cor. 14:1). The Corinthian church was like a poster child for immaturity, and yet Paul was exhorting the members of this fledgling, imperfect church to step out and try their wings. He trusted that the Spirit of God inside each one of the Corinthian believers could prevail over their all-too-human weaknesses.

What must it have been like there in Corinth? I think it must have sounded like a symphony orchestra before the concert begins, when everybody is tuning up and all you can hear is squeaking, tooting, squawking, and thumping. It does not sound very much like the piece of music you will hear in a minute, and yet both times it is the same musicians playing the same instruments. The difference is in the way they respond to the direction of the conductor. If you walked into a meeting of the church in Corinth, I imagine it might have sounded as if somebody had just asked every adult in the room to repeat his or her full name, age, birthday, social security number, address, and phone number all at the same time. Most of them were speaking in tongues loudly. One guy was standing on his chair giving a prophecy. One was trying to give his testimony. Another was turning in circles looking for somebody to pray for. It must have been kind of a zoo.

Paul's instructions to the Corinthians represent the only such instructions in the Bible. He began diplomatically and lovingly, commending them for a few things, for example, *"I praise you because you remember me in everything and hold firmly to the traditions, just as I delivered them to you"* (1 Cor. 11:2). Then he went on to correct and instruct them. There were big problems in this church—divisions and immorality. People were drunk when they came to take communion. During meetings they competed with each other—loudly.

Yet Paul did not say, "Stop doing everything. Shut it all off. Close up shop. This is out of control." Instead, he simply gave instructions on how to "do church" properly. In a way, he was like John the Baptist, preparing the way of the Lord. We need his instructions again today.

Paul gave them an ordered framework to work with. He emphasized mutual sensitivity, proper understanding, and honor and respect for the operations of the Spirit. He taught them how to tune their hearts to the Conductor who was standing in the midst of them.

Various Forms of Revelation

The revelations of the quickened Word come forth in various formats. Inspired worship songs, anointed preaching and teaching, dreams and visions, and the gift of tongues are some of God's modes of expression. Discernment of spirits is also a form of revelation. God speaks in all kinds of ways. But I believe that the most appropriate form of revelation in a public meeting is the corporate prophetic utterance, which can be distinguished from private, personal prophecy. Without getting into a discussion of the "office" of prophet and how that can differ from the gift of prophecy and the spirit of prophecy, I simply want to encourage all believers to explore prophetic expression, particularly in the context of their local church.

Paul wrote to the Corinthians:

> One who speaks in a tongue edifies himself; but one who prophesies edifies the church. Now I wish that you all spoke in tongues, but even more that you would prophesy; and greater is one who prophesies than one who speaks in tongues, unless he interprets, so that the church may receive edifying (1 Corinthians 14:4-5).

Did Paul mean that speaking in tongues is bad? Did he want the people to speak in tongues less? I don't think so. He wanted all of them to speak in tongues. But even more, he wanted all of them to prophesy, or at least to interpret the tongues into the easily-comprehended language of the assembly. The result, he said, would be edification. Paul wanted the church to be edified, that is, to be built up and strengthened.

Some people think that prophecy must predict the future. Sometimes it does, but it can also describe, interpret, and explain something that has happened in the past or something that is going on currently. Sometimes prophecy reveals the condition of people's hearts and provides the ways and means for change.

A prophetic word is not bound by space or time, but it is bound to Jesus' heart. The difference between Christian prophetic ministry and divination or psychic activity (which is non-Christian), is that Christ-centered prophetic ministry reveals the true condition of a person's heart, reveals God's heart, and tells the person what to do about his or her condition, all while lifting up Jesus as the Savior and Healer.

A prophetic word is designed to advance the Church through what I call the "three pillars of prophecy."

Three Pillars of Prophecy

The intention of a prophetic utterance can be to magnify God, as when Mary the mother of Jesus visited her older cousin Elizabeth and she began spontaneously to glorify the Lord's name:

> *My soul magnifies the Lord, and my spirit has rejoiced in God my Savior. For He has regarded the lowly state of His maidservant; for behold, henceforth all generations will call me blessed. For He who is mighty has done great things for*

*me, and holy is His name. And His mercy is
on those who fear Him from generation to generation. He has shown strength with His arm;
He has scattered the proud in the imagination of
their hearts. He has put down the mighty from
their thrones, and exalted the lowly. He has filled
the hungry with good things, and the rich He has
sent away empty. He has helped His servant Israel, in remembrance of His mercy, as He spoke
to our fathers, to Abraham and to his seed forever*
(Luke 1:46-55 NKJV).

That was prophecy. After the children of Israel had
crossed over the Red Sea and Miriam and the people
danced and rejoiced with singing, the song they sang was
prophecy too (see Exod. 15). In a prophetic church, many
prophetic words are delivered for this purpose alone—
magnifying the Lord.

Many other words are direct words of edification
meant to build up the hearers in their faith. Some are
words of loving comfort and reassurance when God just
wants to reveal His love and He chooses to do it prophetically. Still others are words of exhortation, words that
urge and persuade and admonish. These words are not
scoldings, but rather warnings or cautionings: "You need
to stay on this track. Stick to your original vision. Watch
out for danger."

The three pillars of prophecy are *edification, exhortation,* and *comfort.* They compose the threefold purpose
of prophetic ministry according to First Corinthians 14.
The intention of any prophetic word should be to build
people up individually and corporately, to strengthen and
restore the church members and the church body, and to
reflect the nature of God, which is love.

I prefer the word *exhortation* to the word *encouragement,* as it is sometimes translated, because *exhortation*

seems to include a greater breadth of meaning that has to do with entreaty, imploring, persuasiveness, sometimes admonishment and even warning or directive commands. Some people interpret such things negatively. When God says, "You had better watch out," they think God is mad at them. But God's warnings are part of His protectiveness. If my young son is heading into a pasture where a wild bull is grazing, I would say, "Watch out, son. Stop! Don't go there!" I would be emphatic and very directive. It would be out of love and a fatherly protectiveness that I would speak up. Sometimes prophecy can sound like that.

Prophecy reveals the intentions and purposes of God for the corporate church as well as for individuals. Very often, such prophecies are conditional. Their fulfillment depends on the response of the people. Paul wrote to his son in the faith, Timothy:

> *This command I entrust to you, Timothy, my son, in accordance with the prophecies previously made concerning you, that by them you fight the good fight, keeping faith and a good conscience, which some have rejected and suffered shipwreck in regard to their faith* (1 Timothy 1:18-19).

Evidently some people had rejected the prophetic advice and had failed to keep the faith. God had intended to do certain things with them, but they had bailed out. Instead of "fighting the good fight" as Paul was urging Timothy to do, they had fallen by the wayside. To this day, people spurn the living Word all the time. Jesus died for the sins of the whole world, and yet when the end comes, hell will be populated with the people who rejected His message.

We must steward the prophetic message, recognizing that God reveals His blessings for a purpose. When God speaks through a prophet, He intends to get results. He does not speak merely to cheer us up or to give us Holy Ghost goose bumps. He wants to speak into existence His purpose for our lives.

Five Intelligible Words

Paul wrote, *"In the church I would rather speak five intelligible words to instruct others than ten thousand words in a tongue"* (1 Cor. 14:19 NIV). Obviously, he was not concerned about looking "spiritual," which speaking in tongues might have suggested. His single-minded focus was on one thing—building up the Church. He reported that he used the gift of tongues more than anyone he knew, but in a church setting, he preferred to speak God's words in the language that the people could understand.

Paul went on to give guidelines to the Corinthians:

> *Brethren, do not be children in your thinking; yet in evil be infants, but in your thinking be mature.... So then tongues are for a sign, not to those who believe but to unbelievers; but prophecy is for a sign, not to unbelievers but to those who believe. Therefore if the whole church assembles together and all speak in tongues, and ungifted men or unbelievers enter, will they not say that you are mad? But if all prophesy, and an unbeliever or an ungifted man enters, he is convicted by all, he is called to account by all; the secrets of his heart are disclosed; and so he will fall on his face and worship God, declaring that God is certainly among you.*

> *What is the outcome then, brethren? When you assemble, each one has a psalm, has a teaching, has a revelation, has a tongue, has an interpretation. Let all things be done for edification. If*

anyone speaks in a tongue, it should be by two or at the most three, and each in turn, and one must interpret; but if there is no interpreter, he must keep silent in the church; and let him speak to himself and to God. Let two or three prophets speak, and let the others pass judgment. (But if a revelation is made to another who is seated, the first one must keep silent. For you can all prophesy one by one, so that all may learn and all may be exhorted; and the spirits of prophets are subject to prophets; for God is not a God of confusion but of peace, as in all the churches of the saints (1 Corinthians 14:20,22-33).

These are good guidelines, but they are guidelines only, not edicts. They have some latitude; if you have four prophecies (more than *"two or at the most three"*), don't worry; you haven't sinned! Paul did not suggest that each church needs a scorekeeper to keep track of how many times somebody speaks up, nor did he intend to imply that anybody who makes a mistake should be ostracized. He simply portrayed a workable format for a meeting of the church, in which people take turns sharing the words of the Lord, paying attention to each other, and deferring to each other if necessary. When he wrote that *"the spirits of prophets are subject to prophets,"* he was saying that seasoned, proven, experienced prophetic people are the ones who are sensitive enough to be qualified to discern and judge the prophetic ministry in a church.

Along with commending intelligible words of prophecy over words spoken in tongues, Paul urged that messages in tongues should receive interpretation from people who have the spiritual gift of interpretation (which is a variety of a prophetic gift). Interpretation, by the way, is not quite the same as translation. When a person speaks a public message in tongues that is subsequently interpreted, the relative wordiness and apparent sentence structure can be quite different. The interpretation is just that—an interpretation of the meaning of the utterance in tongues. The interpretation may sound like a prophecy or a prayer. The person who receives it has the same kind of "quickening" inside as a prophet does when he or she receives a word. The active anointing or unction of the Holy Spirit releases the word of the Lord.

Paul was not saying that every single time somebody uses the gift of tongues, somebody else must be there to interpret it. He refers only to the use of the gift in public settings, where other people can hear the message. When a person speaks in tongues or uses any other spiritual gift in a public meeting, the person is ministering with a threefold orientation. The person is ministering first to the Lord by means of worship, praise, and exultation. Second, the person is ministering to the other believers in the room. And third, the person is ministering to any unbelievers who are present (and this could include believers who do not yet understand how the gifts of the Spirit operate). This explains the need for sensitivity and discretion.

No offense will be given if somebody prays in tongues under his or her breath or sings in the Spirit when other people are singing the words of a song. But if a person bellows at top volume—whether in tongues or not—a newcomer will be, at the least, confused. Certainly the newcomer will not be edified. Paul's advice: interpret the message so the whole group knows what is happening.

The words of prophecy are more direct. They are readily understandable. In fact, they can convince and convict an unbeliever in a meeting, bringing the person to faith. With the secrets of the heart revealed, he or she will fall down in awe, convinced that God is truly alive and present in the place.

I have been in churches when the prophetic presence of God was so awesome that everybody ended up on the floor. God's power did it, not human hype or pressure or gymnastics. The carpet wasn't low enough. Everybody ended up confessing all of their sins back to kindergarten. And then the presence of God came with tenderness and love and blessing, showering grace on people and showing them how to change.

As we become prophetic people, we will hear more testimonies of what happened when God sent conviction through a prophetic word. This happens to me from time to time. One time I prophesied to a woman who had never been in that particular church before. Little did I know that she was not a believer. When I walked up to her, I saw a question mark over her head, so I said, "You have so many questions," and I began to share the Gospel with her. She went home that day, got saved, and later married a young Christian man. Today they are leaders in the church. She said she was convinced because the secret questions of her heart were revealed and the intents of God's heart were explained to her. That is a good example of how prophecy can work in a public meeting.

A true prophetic word needs to be a "distinct sound" with a distinct meaning so that people can benefit from it. Paul used this analogy:

> *If I come to you speaking in tongues, what will I profit you unless I speak to you either by way of revelation or of knowledge or of prophecy or of teaching? Yet even lifeless things, either flute or harp, in producing a sound, if they do not produce a distinction in the tones, how will it be known what is played on the flute or on the harp? For if the bugle produces an indistinct sound, who will prepare himself for battle? So also you, unless you utter by the tongue speech*

that is clear, how will it be known what is spo-
ken? For you will be speaking into the air. There
are, perhaps, a great many kinds of languages
in the world, and no kind is without meaning. If
then I do not know the meaning of the language,
I will be to the one who speaks a barbarian, and
the one who speaks will be a barbarian to me. So
also you, since you are zealous of spiritual gifts,
seek to abound for the edification of the church
(1 Corinthians 14:6-12).

God's intention is that the spiritual gifts He has be-
stowed on the Church would be used for edification, exhortation, and comfort. That should be the intention of
our hearts as well.

A Matter of Heart Motivation

Do you remember the renowned magician named Simon who met Philip in Samaria? (See Acts 8:9-24.) *"Claim-*
ing to be someone great," he had impressed people with
his feats of magic (Acts 8:9). But when he saw the greater
wonders that Philip and his companions could perform
in the name of Jesus, *"Even Simon himself believed; and*
after being baptized, he continued on with Philip, and as
he observed signs and great miracles taking place, he was
constantly amazed" (Acts 8:13).

The apostles Peter and John arrived in town, and they
began to pray for the newly-baptized Samaritan believers
to receive the Holy Spirit. This was something new. Even
more amazed, Simon wanted to add this specific demonstration of power to his spiritual repertoire. (See Acts
8:14-19.) He viewed it as a commodity to be purchased,
and he offered the apostles cash in exchange for acquir-
ing this authority to bestow the Holy Spirit on other people. Peter was horrified:

*But Peter said to him, "May your silver perish
with you, because you thought you could obtain
the gift of God with money! You have no part or
portion in this matter, for your heart is not right
before God. Therefore repent of this wickedness
of yours, and pray the Lord that, if possible, the
intention of your heart may be forgiven you. For
I see that you are in the gall of bitterness and in
the bondage of iniquity"* (Acts 8:20-23).

Outwardly Simon's desires were honorable. He had
even been baptized as a believer in Jesus. But inwardly
his motives were tainted. He wanted the right thing for
the wrong reason.

Oftentimes that is what we can detect under the surface when we listen to a prophetic message. The words
may be scriptural and true, but something is wrong with
the prophet's motives.

People are far from perfect, and yet God has chosen
to speak through them. God can and will speak through
people who are sinners. He does want us to earnestly
desire the spiritual gifts, especially prophecy. (Remember
First Corinthians 14:1 [NKJV]—*"Pursue love, and desire
spiritual gifts, but especially that you may prophesy."*) Yet
He does not require us to pass a set of exams before we
step up to a microphone.

A person with a humble and obedient heart may be
too timid to speak up, whereas a self-motivated person
may be over-bold, which only makes the problem more
difficult for a church to conquer. We need to address our
heart motives, and we need to be honest about them, loving each other as we grow.

A person who wants to appear to be "spiritual" will
stand up to deliver a prophetic word, and they will have
their reward—having been allowed to speak, they will

have gained a certain amount of recognition. But will the church be edified? I don't think so. The people may say, "Amen!" out of habitual response, but they will not gain anything from the word they just endorsed.

This sensitive matter becomes even stickier when the prophet gives a corrective or a directive word. In such a case, underlying problems include not only heart motives, but also position and governmental authority in a body of believers, as well as timing. People have been blown away when somebody has gotten up and declared, "There is sin in the camp. We need to go on a 90-day fast. Somebody needs to sell his house...." Before any public declaration, all corrective and directive words should be submitted first to the leaders of the church to sort out the wheat from the chaff.

Heart motivations will remain a problem as long as the Church is composed of human beings. The only antidote is a thriving culture of God's love. For good reason, Paul tucked the well-known "love chapter," First Corinthians 13, between chapters 12 and 14, which are so heavily concerned with prophecy and the other spiritual gifts in the Church. Love will outlast prophecy:

> *If I have the gift of prophecy, and know all mysteries and all knowledge; and if I have all faith, so as to remove mountains, but do not have love, I am nothing.... [Love] does not act unbecomingly; it does not seek its own.... Love never fails; but if there are gifts of prophecy, they will be done away; if there are tongues, they will cease; if there is knowledge, it will be done away. For we know in part and we prophesy in part; but when the perfect comes, the partial will be done away.... But now faith, hope, love, abide these three; but the greatest of these is love* (1 Corinthians 13:2, 5, 8-10, 13).

We will only get better at hearing and delivering prophetic words through practice, which includes the refining that comes through making mistakes and receiving correction. The only way we can give—or receive—correction effectively is through love. *"Love covers a multitude of sins"* in our interactions, especially where either party could become offended (see 1 Pet. 4:8).

Coming to Church Prepared to Prophesy

Even with pure, unselfish motives, a person can mistake a personal word from God for one that is supposed to be delivered to the church body. Part of maturing as a prophet is learning the difference.

The best safeguard is to check with somebody else. We all need to grow in our understanding of how the Spirit of God operates, and we need to help each other learn. In a healthy church, people will not be afraid to try something new, and their leaders will not be afraid to correct a problem when it happens.

The goal is always the same—edification. What will build up the body as a whole? The Corinthian church was not yet mature, but Paul considered it healthy enough to be able to receive his instruction. They were underway in the maturation process, and he could hold up goals for them. Paul was writing to a church full of people who were committed to each other. They had experienced each other's spiritual gifts. They loved the Lord, and they had been filled with His Spirit.

So instead of shutting them down because they were immature, Paul held up a vision for them: "See, here is the way to do it, church." He wanted them to allow the Holy Spirit to speak through them, and he knew that a true move of the Spirit would be inviting, exciting, edifying, and orderly all at the same time. Paul helped the

Corinthians visualize how it could be in their church meetings, with each person coming ready to speak up or sing out or simply listen, attentive in their spirits to the Spirit of God: *"When you assemble, each one has a psalm, has a teaching, has a revelation, has a tongue, has an interpretation. Let all things be done for edification"* (1 Cor. 14:26).

Our churches today are supposed to be like that too. Next time you are in church, if you feel the Spirit stirring inside you, do not dismiss it as your imagination. If you have prayed and you are walking with the Lord and now you are in church and feeling God moving, give it a shot. Step out in faith. Get up and share with somebody who is in a leadership role. With an attitude of innocence and expectation, you will be able to receive their confirmation and direction. Until you step out, you will not be very useful.

With practice, your spiritual senses will get sharpened and your spirit, which is your organ of spiritual perception, will expand and mature. The Greek word *aistheterion* is translated as "senses" in Hebrews 5:14, and in that verse discernment is portrayed as the direct result of practice: *"Solid food is for the mature, who because of practice have their senses trained to discern good and evil"* (Heb. 5:14).

At first, you may only receive words that corroborate other words that have been received already. Your "word" may only be the fact that you had a dream last night or that you were reading a particular part of Scripture all week, and it may not be the word that gets shared at all. But that is OK because you will be part of the confirmation of God's word, and you will be learning how to exercise your prophetic senses.

As you exercise your God-given ability to hear His voice, you will begin to find your place in the Body of

Christ, where all the parts work together for the common good.

A Sending Prayer

Living Word of God, may each one of us become a useful vessel for Your Spirit. Increase our faith so that we can know what You want us to do and how You want us to do it. We believe that You want to speak to us through each other and that we need to be willing to hear from You for the sake of others. May we become a prophetic people, and may You regard us as worthy of our calling. We are asking for Your favor and blessing as we deliver Your Word, in the name of the Anointed One, glorifying Your name now and always. Amen.

Chapter 7

Prophetic Initiative, Prophetic Etiquette

"The prophetic" is not some side dish that we serve to impress people with our giftedness. It is not like a little extra whipped cream on your ice cream sundae. It is the radical finger of God pointing—*"This is the way, walk in it"* (Isa. 30:21). Prophetic words reveal God's heart to the people He has called His Body on the earth, identifying and shaping the Church with edification, encouragement, exhortation, and comfort.

"The prophetic" is the Lord of the Church taking the initiative to say:

> *Do not fear, for I have redeemed you; I have called you by name; you are Mine! When you pass through the waters, I will be with you; and through the rivers, they will not overflow you. When you walk through the fire, you will not be scorched, nor will the flame burn you. For I am the Lord your God, the Holy One of Israel, your Savior.... I am the Lord, I have called You in*

righteousness, I will also hold You by the hand and watch over You, and I will appoint You as a covenant to the people, as a light to the nations, to open blind eyes, to bring out prisoners from the dungeon and those who dwell in darkness from the prison (Isaiah 43:1-3; 42:6-7).

Prophetic Initiative

Without God's prophetic initiative, the Church cannot flourish. Like a loving Bridegroom, He wants to encourage and sustain His intended Bride. The Church is the Bride of Christ, and I do not know any man who is engaged to be married who would bad-mouth his fiancé. A man would not be engaged for much longer if he spoke unkindly to her or issued ultimatums or slapped her around, would he? What if he said, "If you don't straighten up I am breaking this thing off"? What a great way to start a marriage.

No, even when He speaks sternly, the Bridegroom speaks with wisdom and love. When He sees a need to straighten something out, He does it in a way that does not leave the Church in a hopeless condition. He leads her and guides her. The whole point of the prophetic ministry is God's initiative to build up the Bride of Christ spiritually and morally, to comfort the people who honor His name, and to open doors to Heaven.

When the believer named Ananias opened the door to the house on Straight Street where Saul was staying (see Acts 9), Saul, who had been blinded by God on the road to Damascus, looked up toward the sound. He could not see his visitor, but he heard these words, "Brother Saul...." Ananias, who until the Lord had spoken to him had not considered Saul a brother but rather a dangerous enemy of the Church, proceeded to tell Saul why God had blinded him on the road and more. In fact Ananias's prophetic words confirmed in detail everything about Paul's future ministry, and when he finished speaking, Paul's blinded eyes were able to see again, and he got baptized even before taking his first meal as a Christ-follower. That's what I call a good example of the prophetic initiative!

Much later, certain prophets and teachers were gathered at Antioch to seek the Lord (see Acts 13:1-2). While they were praying, God spoke prophetically to indicate that Saul and Barnabas should be set apart for a missionary trip. Probably half of the guys in the room were qualified to go on such a trip, but the Spirit took the initiative to speak through someone to point out these particular two. The group concurred. The Holy Spirit was directing their decisions. He was (as He should be for the Church today) the Chief Executive of the Body of Christ, and (now as then) He uses prophetic means to communicate with the people of the Body.

You see, prophecy is meant not only to supply encouragement and perspective and life for the internal life of the Church. Prophetic initiative causes the individuals in a local church to *do* something, and most of the time, prophetic words send them outside of the church to do it. Not only does the Spirit send people on missionary journeys, He commissions them for mundane, everyday things as well. He takes the initiative to tell them what to do, and He equips them to do it.

Too many churches for too many years have missed the boat regarding God's prophetic initiatives. I don't think you can blame God when a church of 5,000 members decides to keep its doors closed to the outside world. That congregation will manage to keep their kids in there from birth until graduation with their state-of-the-art sound system and their gymnasium, but what will they have to show for it? How many times will they have to ignore the radical, world-loving word of the Lord to maintain their fortress mentality? How many times will they have misinterpreted His initiatives?

The Spirit of God is looking for people who will listen to Him. *"The eyes of the Lord run to and fro throughout the whole earth, to show Himself strong on behalf of those whose heart is loyal to Him..."* (2 Chron. 16:9 NKJV). If you are one of the people who have been sensing His stirrings, you may need to be a Caleb or a Joshua, waiting, patient, but alert for the times to change, not discouraged by an evil report, but sure of what you have heard from your God. You may need to declare in prayer that if God wants to do something, you will volunteer for duty. You may need to prophesy to your obstacles and follow closely as your Lord tells you what to do.

You can prophesy over your own life and initiate change. I know a couple who could not have children; they were barren, although they had received prophetic words about having children. So they began to prophesy over their own bodies and their own circumstances. They started going around their house singing over their barrenness, confessing the word of God—until something changed. The doctor who had said they would not be able to have any children was privileged to deliver their baby.

You can prophesy to the devil too; did you realize that? That's what David did when he confronted Goliath. David had learned to hear God's voice, so he was not afraid to say, *"The Lord who delivered me from the paw of the lion and from the paw of the bear, He will deliver me from the hand of this Philistine"* (1 Sam. 17:37). He took the initiative when all of the better-equipped and better-trained soldiers did not. He was so sure that the Lord was with him that he did not wait for the giant to hurl his spear first, but instead he ran toward him, his own prophetic words still ringing in the air:

*This day the Lord will deliver you up into my
hands, and I will strike you down and remove
your head from you. And I will give the dead bodies of the army of the Philistines this day to the
birds of the sky and the wild beasts of the earth,
that all the earth may know that there is a God in
Israel, and that all this assembly may know that
the Lord does not deliver by sword or by spear;
for the battle is the Lord's and He will give you
into our hands* (1 Samuel 17:46-47).

God's words, expressed prophetically, are meant to accomplish something. That is why He takes the initiative to express them using the voices of His servants who take the initiative to follow through in obedience.

Living Words From Living Stones

In the words of the Bible, the members of the Body of Christ have been compared to "living stones" who are *"be-ing built up as a spiritual house"* (1 Pet. 2:5). I believe that one of the reasons God designed the Church this way is so that we would have to be humble and rely on one an-other. We are not isolated stones scattered around on the ground. We need to lean on each other, and we need to hold each other up.

The prophetic words we bring to each other are part of our life together. They are meant to bring life, God's life, to people and situations that tend to become chaotic. True prophecy reveals people's hearts, and it reveals the heart of God. It also reveals a God-directed solution. Most prophecy confirms what the Lord has already been show-ing people anyway, but it inspires its hearers to open their hearts anew to the life-giving Christ.

That is why true prophecy is not just Christian fortune-telling. Occult prophecy can tell you what you did when you were a kid, whom you are going to marry, your name, address, and cell phone number. But a living word that comes from the living God, a word spoken through a fallible but living "stone," brings life. It may be misinterpreted in the delivery or in the reception. It may be added to or subtracted from. But a true prophetic word will help to build the Body. It will express life because the prophetic people who bring the words have prophetic lives, not merely prophetic gifts.

Now let's shift the analogy from living stones to living plants: It is true that green, growing things get a little disorderly sometimes. If you don't tend your garden, you can have a jungle before you know it. For that reason, Paul addressed the Corinthian church with corrective words regarding their out-of-control expression of spiritual gifts in meetings. But he did not correct them so severely that the life died out. By his instruction that people should do everything *"decently and in order"* (1 Cor. 14:40 NKJV), he did not intend to make the church resemble a cemetery, where everyone is lined up in rows, nice and neat and tidy—and dead.

However, he did intend to indicate some "prophetic protocol," some practical tools for prophetic behavior that would make it easier, not harder, for the living word of God to do its life-producing work in the Church.

Moving Together in the Spirit

Since the prophetic word is meant to build up the Body of Christ, and since the Body of Christ is made up of many dissimilar individuals who are at various stages of spiritual growth, we need to learn how to move together in the Spirit.

The overall goal of prophetic protocol is to supply practical rules that can make it possible for the people of

God to develop *corporate sensitivity* to His Spirit. All the "rules" that we can learn from the Bible and from firsthand experience should be oriented around this objective.

Corporate sensitivity involves attentiveness, first and foremost, to God's voice. But it also involves attentiveness to each other. It is like ballroom dancing, and God is leading. His dancing partner, His Bride, needs to practice to gain the level of sensitivity she needs to respond smoothly to His subtle signals. Not only must she decline to take the lead herself, all the parts of her body must become coordinated so that she can follow her Companion. In a way, she must learn to dance "by faith" more than by sight, sensing her partner's movement with her entire body.

When the Holy Spirit is moving, sometimes the whole Body will feel it. They will know that they all need to wait quietly and expectantly—or rise to their feet with shouts and applause. Sometimes the corporate sensitivity can be hard to detect. It will be as subtle as an inner surge of affirmation when someone gets up to make a statement or read a Scripture. The more we "tune in" when we are together, the more we will enjoy the unity of heart that will enable us to really say "Amen!" and mean it.

Appropriateness

Certain things are appropriate; certain things are not. When a spirit of prophecy begins to stir in an assembly, it is not the right time to stand up and give your testimony about how God paid your $10,000 phone bill. You may be quite excited about it, and naturally it will give glory to God when you tell the story, but right then, it does not fit.

To achieve corporate sensitivity, each individual needs to grow in sensitivity to the Spirit and to "learn the ropes" of spiritual etiquette for that particular group. We run the danger of interrupting the Lord; we do not want to cut Him off. Once the meeting is out of His flow, it can be nearly impossible to get back into it again.

Rest assured, if you are meant to share a word publicly, God will prevail. With experience, you can learn how to gauge the level of importance and the timing along with the appropriateness for the setting. One time I was in a meeting in another city with a lot of leaders in attendance. While a highly respected leader was teaching, I felt that God gave me a clear word. Because it was such a big meeting and I was not from the area, I was intimidated and so I hesitated. I let it slip by. Then it was time for the main speaker to teach, and the first 35 minutes of his teaching consisted of everything I had heard from God. It would have been such a faith-builder for him as well as for the whole group if I had dared to give the word earlier. I had to work my way out from under a pile of condemnation for that one, but I did learn one thing: God is not going to kill me or think I am a bad person for not responding to Him. He just wanted to encourage us. I would still rather be lovingly sensitive than brazenly over-confident, but I learned to let God prevail over my timidity a little bit more after that.

Personal or Corporate?

There is a difference between a personal word and a corporate word. Sometimes you will hear God speaking, but what He is saying does not apply to anyone else. He is speaking to you privately. It can be hard to tell the difference, because God may reveal something to you that is very clear, and you might think that everyone would benefit from hearing your wonderful revelation. Sometimes they might, but not always. You need to ask Him whether or not you should try to share it. Over time, you will grow in your discernment and sensitivity as to what to do with a word that you receive from God in a corporate setting.

Check It Out

Before standing up to say something, you can always check with those who are leading a meeting. They should be able to both witness to the content of your word as well as to the timing of your delivery. Some churches have a rule about this, and I can respect that when I am worshiping with them, even though my church does not. For someone with a strong track record in a committed relationship, a look and a nod indicates permission to proceed. In other fellowships, the "checker" will ask simple questions about the nature or context of the prophetic word about to be given.

I think it is interesting that in our church, the people who are the most trustworthy happen to be the ones who are the most willing to submit their words to the leaders. These people are proven prophets. They always have good things to say, never anything weird. Needless to say, they always get the green light from the leadership. Therefore, you would think that they would stop checking with the leaders before sharing a word. But they value corporate sensitivity so they get their words checked out. We do not make this a requirement, but these people consider it helpful.

Others—the ones who would be offended if we did create a rule about checking with the authorities before prophesying—often end up giving off-the-wall words that do not help anybody.

In some larger churches, random public prophecy is not permitted at all. They have proven prophets on the scene, and they instruct people to have the pastor or a prophet speak forth words that the Lord may have given to others. This helps avoid situations in which a single tainted prophecy could devastate immature listeners. This approach can allow prophetic liberty as long as those in charge can sustain the extra effort involved.

Tune In

Pray for precision during the prophetic flow. Tune your heart in to the Spirit of the Lord. Pray for others to be able to tune in too and for them to overcome any obstacles to receiving words from God during the meeting. You may never know how important your prayers were. This is part of allowing the Holy Spirit to be in control of the meeting, and it is part of His making us more excellent in what we do together. If the whole congregation can get a sense of the prophetic flow, the impact is far greater than if only a few prophetic people get illumination.

Avoid "Stealth Prophecies"

Prophetic words differ from each other in their orientation. Some are directive words or even words of correction. Others are words of comfort, wisdom, commendation, or good basic spiritual advice. Some churches will not allow anyone except established, trusted prophets to deliver words that are directive or corrective. This is for the protection of the rest of the Body.

When people take it upon themselves to waylay others and say, "God is telling me such-and-such about you," or "I had this dream about you last night," we have a name for it. We call those "parking lot prophecies" or "bathroom prophecies" because of where they most often occur. We don't endorse that approach. Words of direction or correction have a powerful impact, and we do not want to risk ruining someone by approving an "anything goes" policy.

We especially need to warn against prophetic words that strongly affect the lives of individuals and families, such as directives to change jobs, marry (or divorce), buy or sell, and so forth. Such decisions should never hinge on a single prophetic word.

A related restriction is for the protection of guest speakers and leaders: Do not take it upon yourself to approach them with a "special word." Instead, share such words with a third party who can discern the appropriateness of conveying the message to its intended recipient. Each fellowship needs to develop its own guidelines that are appropriate for how personal prophetic words should be shared in the context of a public gathering.

Another helpful constraint: No "cockroach prophecies," the kind that come out in the dark, the ones that are dark, negative, unbridled, often opinionated words delivered in the guise of prophetic style. It is not that God cannot warn, admonish, and rebuke through a prophetic word, but when God does it, people feel convicted, and He tells them how to obtain victory—rather than making them feel condemned and hopeless.

Once in a while, people take advantage of a public platform to broadcast their opinions. This is not prophetic revelation, and it can carry a harsh and critical tone. In such situations, leaders have a responsibility to speak up. Without becoming quarrelsome, a leader can publicly correct the situation, thus guarding the hearts and minds of God's people, and then privately deal with the individual later. In over 30 years of church leadership, I have had to do this only one time. It is not a pleasant task, but it is part of shepherding God's people. We must have a healthy fear of the Lord and a strong sense of honor about how we allow His people to be influenced.

On the other hand, words of general edification or exhortation can be received by almost anyone without negative repercussions. Again, corporate sensitivity is the key to knowing what to do. As we tune in to God and look out for each other's well-being, our corporate sensitivity will improve steadily. Ask yourself the question that Paul posed in his letter to the Corinthians: *"What is the outcome then, brethren? When you assemble, each one has a psalm, has a teaching, has a revelation, has a tongue, has an interpretation. Let all things be done for edification"* (1 Cor. 14:26). Cultivate a heart that wants to build up the Body of Christ.

"Comprehend With All the Saints"

As we mature individually and corporately, everything that we bring forth at a meeting will help us to unveil the glory of Jesus. Paul wrote this to the church at Ephesus:

> *For this reason I bow my knees to the Father of our Lord Jesus Christ, from whom the whole family in heaven and earth is named, that He would grant you, according to the riches of His glory, to be strengthened with might through His Spirit in the inner man, that Christ may dwell in your hearts through faith; that you, being rooted and grounded in love, may be able to* **comprehend with all the saints** what is the width and length and depth and height—to know the love of Christ which passes knowledge; that you may be filled with all the fullness of God (Ephesians 3:14-19 NKJV).

The word *comprehend* in the Greek is *katalambano*, and it means to apprehend, to take hold of eagerly, to attain, to find, to perceive, to understand. This does not occur through deductive reasoning. It has to happen through spiritual revelation.

In a mature prophetic church, the teachings, the psalms, the prophetic words, and the testimonies will work together to bring the people into the fullness of Christ Jesus, and they will comprehend more about Him. They will become more sensitive to His voice. They will begin to understand the purposes of God. They will be able to bear fruit for the Kingdom.

I am looking forward to the day when the local churches will be moving together in the Spirit, when it is commonplace for the day's teaching to get confirmed by the music that the worship leader chooses along with prophetic sharings from a dozen people, dreams, visions, words, Scripture readings, and more from the prophetic people of God.

How Does It Work?

When a prophetic flow begins to move in a meeting, the people who are sensitive to the Spirit can tell that the Lord is about to do something. That is the right time to pray that others will get into the flow and not quench it. The flow can get closed off too quickly. Somebody may start a song or stand up to give a testimony just when it was time for a prophetic word. It may be the case that the people who choose to start a song or whatever are feeling the same stirrings, but they just didn't know what to do with them. Sometimes it seems to me that the "pregnant pause" times get filled up before the prophetic people can respond. It makes me want to urge them to hurry up.

While it is easy to become incongruent with the flow of the Spirit, it is also possible to get better at receiving, discerning, and delivering a word. Here is how it usually works:

First, you feel something welling up in your spirit. Sometimes a word or a picture comes into your mind.

Sometimes it is a particular theme, perhaps only a sense that God desires to express Himself. For some people, this happens before a meeting, and they may have an additional sense about when to deliver the word, or they may just hold onto the word (or often the partial word) until they sense a quickening, an anointing, or an "unction" in their spirits.

When you feel it is time to speak (perhaps at the discretion of a leader you have consulted), you do not have to add, "thus saith the Lord." Neither does your word have to be delivered in King James English—unless you are trained and flow in that type of prophetic language, which would make it normal and natural for you. Special words will not make what you say into a prophecy. You will develop and become fluent in the Spirit just as people have a regional accent or dialect.

You might deliver the word in the first person, as if you are God Himself. But more often, you will simply explain something to the people. When Peter spoke to the people on the day of Pentecost (see Acts 2), that was a prophetic word. He was filled with the Spirit, suddenly infused with power, and he got an extended revelation about what had just happened. So he explained to the people that this was what the prophet Joel had predicted, and so forth. He was talking to people who knew who Joel was; they were familiar with Joel's prophecy (see Joel 2:28-32). He was persuading his listeners that the hundred-plus people who had been in the upper room were certainly not drunk, but that this, rather, was the outpouring Joel had prophesied about so long before. The Holy Spirit inspired (breathed into) Peter's spirit, and he could explain everything clearly—so clearly that about 3,000 of the people gave their lives to Jesus on the spot (see Acts 2:41).

"In Proportion to Your Faith"

Paul's advice to the people in the church in Rome was to offer public prophetic words to the degree that their faith could support:

> *So we, being many, are one body in Christ, and individually members of one another. Having then gifts differing according to the grace that is given to us, let us use them: if prophecy, let us prophesy in proportion to our faith* (Romans 12:5-6 NKJV).

Our faith gives us courage to step out as well as a sense of "when." When a prophetic word bubbles up inside, it is almost as if somebody has flipped over a three-minute egg timer. The word is ready to go in a certain window of time. You probably know what it feels like to miss the window. You may tremble. You may find a number of things going through your mind, and you wonder if God is trying to say something. You may think, "Why doesn't somebody say something right now?" If nobody steps into the gap, it could be because you were supposed to do it.

The first time you fail to speak up or you fumble around when you do, you may feel like a false prophet or a complete idiot. You may be so embarrassed you wish the earth could swallow you up. (That's better than being one of those people who step up to the microphone without a qualm—usually too often—and who do not seem to understand what it means to take all of their cues from the Holy Spirit.)

Just talk it over with the Holy Spirit and maybe with a trusted friend who was present. Get God's perspective. He will not be as hard on you as you are on yourself. Get past your fears with His help, and keep immersing yourself in His Word.

Cultivate your personal relationship with the Lord above all. He will help you mature to flow in a "custom fit" way prophetically, and He will help you understand where your gift fits into the local Body. Not everyone is meant to deliver glorious words from Heaven in front of hundreds or thousands of listeners. Ask Him to position you where He wants you and to match your faith to what He wants you to do.

Remember that the gifts of God are no measure of character and maturity. In fact, the prophetic gifts (and other gifts) can remain operational even when people fall into serious sin *"for the gifts and the calling of God are irrevocable"* (Rom. 11:29). It seems to me that the fruits of the Spirit, which define character (see Gal. 5:22-23), require just as much of the power of the Holy Spirit as the ability to raise the dead!

Stir Yourself Up

Years ago, I had been invited to a leadership meeting. Sitting there in a roomful of people I regarded as fathers in the Lord, apostles and prophets and church-planters, I intended to keep quiet, mind my own business, and just absorb what was being said. Suddenly an older man, someone who had mentored me personally, walked behind me. He leaned over and said, "Son, stir yourself up."

I needed that, and I did it. As it turned out, the Lord gave me a prophecy during our worship time, and the word helped to set the course for the evening. It was a corporate word that went along with the speaker's message, and it built everyone up.

So now it is my turn to remind you. When you come into a church meeting, stir yourself up. Make yourself open and available to the Holy Spirit. Tell Him, "Lord, I want You to use me."

You may feel that you should pray for others to stir themselves up too. Early in the meeting, look around and pray for whomever catches your attention. You might be surprised, as I have been, to see them step forward in the power of the Spirit later in the meeting. The church will never be edified as God wants it to be if people do not stir themselves up to respond to His movements.

As you remain alert to God throughout the meeting, you may find a certain theme coming back to mind. Perhaps you will remember something you read earlier in the week. You may find a few words or phrases coming into your mind repeatedly, or you may think of a particular verse in the Bible. (I hope you realize that the act of reading Scripture aloud is very prophetic if you are reading under the inspiration of the Spirit.)

You may find yourself praying for others under the Lord's prophetic inspiration. I did this for years before I realized that it was prophetic. I just thought I was praying for people. Right in the middle, the words would take on new significance and often go in a new direction, and the person I was praying with would begin to cry or tell me that I had just prayed for something important.

If you forget to stir yourself up, somebody else might remind you. One time, Barbara and I went to an evening meeting in another church, but we were not there to minister. In fact, we had hired a babysitter because we had a Friday night off, and we were out on a date. I was relaxing in the back, watching somebody else minister. Suddenly he looked over at me and he said, "Do you have a word for this man?" My mind was erased, zero, flatland. I stared back at him. He said, "Yes, you do have a word for this man. Please come here." So I got up and walked over, but I really did not have a clue what to do. I put my hand on the man and opened my mouth and instantly the word of the Lord began to flow. In fact, the man began to vibrate as if he had been plugged into a wall socket. I had had nothing to begin with, but God honored the man who said I had a word.

The whole time it is a walk of faith, and it is all about blessing people. Stir up your love as well as your faith and gifts. Look for feedback from the Lord and remain teachable. It is so much more about Him than it is about you. What a privilege it is to serve Him!

Going With the Flow

Oftentimes, you will find that other spiritual gifts enter into the prophetic flow, such as a word of knowledge or a word of wisdom. It takes practice to learn to discern what is happening in the flow of the Spirit because *"the wind blows where it wishes..."* (John 3:8). The Spirit can manifest His presence in a number of ways.

In an atmosphere of expectancy, worship, and faith, miracles can happen. A word of knowledge does not need to be announced as such ("I am now about to deliver a Word of Knowledge..."). You can simply say something about what the Lord has shown you ("Somebody here has been on dialysis and is scheduled for a kidney transplant...."). The word of knowledge does not heal anybody, but faith rises in response to it, and healing happens by faith.

Faith is much more than a word on a page—it is one of the power gifts (see 1 Cor. 12:9). The spirit of revelation that flows through prophetic utterances releases faith (refer back to Chapter 3). The revelation that comes when the Spirit's flow is strong will release faith, not only for healing, but also for people to step into new areas of ministry, to resist temptation, and more. People who have become discouraged and who feel empty get built up by prophetic ministry. Thanks to their brothers and sisters who have ministered prophetically, they can once again hold out their hands to the Lord and receive from Him.

God knows that some people need outside help even to pray. Others can step into the flow of the Spirit at home through personal journaling and private times with the Lord. Everyone needs to know what the wind of the Spirit feels like so that they can persevere in a life of faith day after day and so that they can turn and minister to others. The prophetic flow of the Spirit can inspire you to pray a specific prayer or call someone on the phone or write a note of blessing. Obedience to the Spirit's suggestions is a very practical outgrowth of spiritual sensitivity.

Freedom in Submission

"Now the Lord is the Spirit, and where the Spirit of the Lord is, there is liberty" (2 Cor. 3:17). This could have been translated, "Where the Spirit is Lord, there is liberty." In other words, whenever we allow the Holy Spirit to be in charge, we are truly free. We are only as free as we yield ourselves to Him.

Part of yielding to Him is submitting to one another. Paul wrote, *"Submit to one another out of reverence for Christ"* (Eph. 5:21 NIV). We need to have a healthy and loving honor and respect for God's authority as it is expressed through His anointed sons and daughters. This does not give us carte blanche to control and manipulate each other. None of us should allow our human spirits to be ruled by another human spirit (even if the other person seems to speak prophetically, saying, "God says you should do such-and-such").

Every personal prophetic word should be submitted first to your own discernment and then to someone else's. If your spirit and the other person's do not bear witness to the word, then let it fall to the ground. If your own spirit and the spirits of others do confirm that the word is genuine, then the best thing you can do is to put more faith in God and rejoice that He has taken the initiative to speak to you.

Responding to the Holy Spirit

When God speaks, there is always a response. The response may not be positive, but it will be a response just the same. One response is to hear the word and commit yourself to it. Or you can hear it clearly—only to remain passive and unmoved. Another response is to reject the word of the Lord or to fight against it. Another response, of course, is to miss hearing the word altogether, which is, sadly, easy to do.

When your response is a positive one, your faith leaps up. The word of God will seem like a "now" word, and you will welcome it. God's word is eternal, and He exists in an eternal "now." Even if it is a predictive word that will not be fulfilled for years, the simple fact that your spirit bears witness to it will increase your faith enough to carry you through the preparation stage.

As you receive the word by faith, you are planting a seed. That is the beginning of fulfillment. And yet, just as with any seed that is planted, many things can threaten its growth. You need to be on the alert for the vision-robber, the devil. You were not the only one who heard that word, you know. The demons in the spirit world heard it too. They heard the prophecies about Jesus, and they caused the killing of a lot of babies (see Matt. 2:16). They caused death and mayhem, but they missed the seed of the move of God. Similarly, as you endure opposition and obey the Lord, a true word from God will grow anyway.

One friend put it this way, "When God speaks, every earth-shaking, mind-blowing, soul-wrenching thing that you could imagine will happen." Sometimes the very opposite of what God said seems to happen. This is not entirely bad. God will use the shaking as a time of testing and strengthening. Sometimes He can form us better in the furnace of affliction. Whenever you feel like a red-hot piece of iron in hot coals, God is holding you like a blacksmith, forming His prophetic intention in your life.

Toward Fruitfulness

The true word of the Lord always bears fruit. He sends His words because He intends for them to accomplish something. Just as He sends the rain and snow down from the sky to water the earth so that it can flourish, not merely to make mud, so He sends His word to initiate a process that leads to a fruitful outcome.

Our participation in that process is important, in that we can enhance or inhibit growth. But the word itself is alive. If something inhibits its growth here, God will re-deposit it through someone else over there. Even with human flaws, He can get across what He wants. He is in control. When you cooperate with His initiatives, you become a participant with Him: *"We have the prophetic word made more sure, to which you do well to pay attention as to a lamp shining in a dark place, until the day dawns and the morning star arises in your hearts"* (2 Pet. 1:19).

A Sending Prayer

Lord, we have a lot to learn, but we are willing students. We thank You for Your continuous help day after day and year after year. We thank You for inspiring faith in our hearts so that we can respond positively to Your stated intentions.

Help us to identify ways we can stir up the prophetic gifts You have given us, and show us how to flow with Your Spirit in both private and corporate settings. Increase our sensitivity to Your voice of direction. We do not want to lean on our own understanding anymore.

Instead we want to glorify You by responding to Your initiatives. We want to bring honor to You. Lead us, teach us, fortify our spirits. We want to participate with You in producing Kingdom fruit on the earth, and we want to do it in collaboration with others who name Your Name. Amen.

Chapter 8

The Power of Prophetic Worship

The one ministry that we are going to continue doing forever is the ministry of worship. The Lord has set eternity in our hearts, and worship opens the way to His throne.

Engaged in worship, we bypass the realm that we are accustomed to, the physical realm of the five senses, our intellects and emotions, and we tap into the spiritual realm. We reach into an invisible place and lay hold of something from our heavenly future that we can bring back into our lives right now. Sometimes we can catch a few notes of the theme that is on the Lord's heart. We can hear what He is saying.

Prophetically speaking, I have probably heard from God more often when I am worshiping than any other time. Nothing and no one can move my heart the way the Lord can, and nothing can open up my heart to His touch as well as worship.

You know as well as I do that this is not just an emotional reaction to some stirring music. Of course our emotions get involved in worship, but it is a lot more than that. In worship, the One who created our emotions and intellects and five senses touches us with His pure love. When someone who really loves you touches you, you want more of it. You feel healthy and free. Joy rises up inside. You want to follow Him at all costs.

A Voice Like Niagara Falls

We can find the best picture of worship in the Book of Revelation. The apostle John had been exiled to an island called Patmos, and he was spending the Lord's Day praying and worshiping, most likely without music. He wrote that he was *"in the Spirit on the Lord's Day"* (Rev. 1:10 NKJV). He was not expecting what happened.

Suddenly behind him he heard an authoritative voice telling him to write messages for seven churches. He turned to see who was speaking. Here is John's report of what he saw and heard:

> *Then I turned to see the voice that spoke with me. And having turned I saw seven golden lampstands, and in the midst of the seven lampstands One like the Son of Man, clothed with a garment down to the feet and girded about the chest with a golden band. His head and hair were white like wool, as white as snow, and His eyes like a flame of fire; His feet were like fine brass, as if refined in a furnace, and His voice as the sound of many waters; He had in His right hand seven stars, out of His mouth went a sharp two-edged sword, and His countenance was like the sun shining in its strength. And when I saw Him, I fell at His feet as dead. But He laid His right hand on me, saying to me, "Do not be afraid; I am the First and the Last. I am He who lives, and was dead, and behold, I am alive forevermore. Amen. And I have the keys*

of Hades and of Death. Write the things which you have seen, and the things which are, and the things which will take place after this (Revelation 1:12-19 NKJV).

This "Son of Man" was Jesus. John had known Jesus better than anybody alive, and yet he had never seen Him looking or sounding like *this*. This was almost beyond description. It literally knocked John off his feet.

John had been part of the intimate three—Peter, James, and John—and he had been present at the most important events that had occurred during Jesus' time on Earth, including the other-worldly transfiguration experience. He was the only one of the 12 disciples who was present at the foot of the cross during the crucifixion, and he had seen the empty tomb with his own eyes three days later. He had watched Jesus ascend into Heaven, and he had been present on the day of Pentecost when the Holy Spirit came like tongues of fire. He had been anointed over and over with His Holy Spirit, more times than he could count, and he had performed miracles as he helped shepherd the new Church for its first decades. Now an elderly man, John had been subjected to inhumane persecution for his tenacious and contagious faith.

In spite of his lengthy resumé as the beloved servant of the Lord Jesus, this revelation of his friend and master Jesus was nothing like the other times. Before John's startled eyes stood the King of Glory, whose voice sounded like "many waters." (If you have ever stood next to Niagara Falls, you may have some idea of the deafening sound level.) This was the Commander of the Universe. His demeanor was startling, blazing, fierce, impossible to look at. He had a warrior's sword coming out of His mouth! John could not take it. He knew the One he had been worshiping, but he honestly did not know that this was going to be on the other side of his worship.

"I Want You to Write It Down"

The Lord touched His old friend John and said, "Do not be afraid." He did not want John to be so fearful that he could not receive the lengthy, imminent revelation. "Write down what you see," Jesus indicated, "and what you see will concern times past, present, and future." As He proceeded to give John some messages for seven churches—real churches filled with real people in specific geographical locations in what is now modern Turkey—the Lord took John deeper into the prophetic realm than he had ever been before. John was just trying to take it all in, to write it all down.

To all of the churches, the Lord blended commendations and exhortations. In essence, He told them, "If you do this...you can overcome." Through John as His prophetic messenger, the Lord Jesus wanted those churches to hear what the Spirit had to say to them. In the same way, He wants us to hear what the Spirit has to say to us today. He wanted them to overcome by the power of the Spirit. He wants the same for us today. He wanted them—and us—to know that there was still a little time left and that mercy was still available.

A Door Standing Open in Heaven

After completing the messages to the seven churches, the Spirit took John deeper still. From chapter 4 of the Book of Revelation, we read what John recorded:

After these things I looked, and behold, a door standing open in heaven. And the first voice which I heard was like a trumpet speaking with me, saying, "Come up here, and I will show you things which must take place after this."

Immediately I was in the Spirit; and behold, a throne set in heaven, and One sat on the throne.

And He who sat there was like a jasper and a sardius stone in appearance; and there was a rainbow around the throne, in appearance like an emerald. Around the throne were twenty-four thrones, and on the thrones I saw twenty-four elders sitting, clothed in white robes; and they had crowns of gold on their heads. And from the throne proceeded lightnings, thunderings, and voices.... And in the midst of the throne, and around the throne, were four living creatures full of eyes in front and in back.... And they do not rest day or night, saying: "Holy, holy, holy, Lord God Almighty, who was and is and is to come!"

Whenever the living creatures give glory and honor and thanks to Him who sits on the throne, who lives forever and ever, the twenty-four elders fall down before Him who sits on the throne and worship Him who lives forever and ever, and cast their crowns before the throne, saying: "You are worthy, O Lord, to receive glory and honor and power...." (Revelation 4:1-6, 8-11 NKJV).

We see that there are different levels of spiritual revelation. Already John had been "in the Spirit on the Lord's Day" and then he makes a point of saying that he was "in the Spirit" anew. Already as he was worshiping, he had heard a voice like many waters, and he had seen an open vision of the glorious Lord in which he heard specific words for named churches. Then he looked up and saw a door standing open in Heaven. In response to the invitation, "Come up here," I believe John actually went somewhere. He did not behold the throne and all the living creatures in a vision; instead he really went there. He went up to another place that was definitely not on the Isle of Patmos.

John had been worshiping before, but his earlier worship was only a shadow of *this* worship. Around the throne, the dynamic, thunderous worship surged in waves. Every time the 24 elders heard the word *holy!* they fell down and took off their crowns of glory and threw them at the feet of the One they were worshiping.

The scene is almost unimaginable, yet one thing we can take away from it is the spiritual power of responding to the call to worship. The more we respond to His holiness, the more we will come out of self-centeredness and self-concern. The more we worship, the more we will be caught up with the drama of Heaven, energized and compelled or propelled by the worship into the prophetic realm. That is certainly what happened for John because he was prepared when the time came for even more revelation of God's words.

"I Saw a Scroll"

He looked at God, seated on His throne, and John saw a scroll in His right hand that was written on both sides and sealed with seven seals (see Rev. 5:1). And when a "strong angel" (who must have been an exceptionally strong angel, since *all* angels are "strong" by definition) asked for a volunteer worthy enough to open the seals on the scroll, *"no one in heaven or on the earth or under the earth was able to open the scroll, or to look at it"* (Rev. 5:3 NKJV).

John's response was explosive. He burst out with loud weeping, which is a form of intercession. No one else seems to have responded this way. John, the man from Earth, moved by the Holy Spirit, was beseeching someone to step forward. This is fitting because when God designed the universe He chose to move through human beings. He even chose to send His Son as a man. Whenever He dispatches an angel with a message, the angel delivers it to a person, and that person must repeat the message prophetically so that it will happen.

John was the only human being on the scene, and his spirit responded forcefully, his travail audible to everyone. One of the 24 elders spoke to him, *"Do not weep. Behold, the Lion of the tribe of Judah, the Root of David, has prevailed to open the scroll and to loose its seven seals"* (Rev. 5:5 NKJV). Someone was going to be able to open the scroll. But who would that be?

John, through the tears in his eyes, saw a Lamb in the midst of the living creatures and elders, next to the One on the throne. The Lamb looked as though it had been slain, yet He lived. He came and put His hand on the scroll (see Rev. 5:6-7).

Worship, Prayer, and the Prophetic Release

Immediately we see even more evidence of the effect that worship and prayerful intercession have in Heaven. As soon as the Lamb took hold of the scroll, the elders and the four living creatures fell down before Him in worship that was greater than before. Each one of the 28 of them was holding *"a harp, and golden bowls full of incense, which are the prayers of the saints"* (Rev. 5:8 NKJV). With the harps in one hand, representing worship, and the bowls of prayer/incense in the other, they sang a new prophetic song:

> *You are worthy to take the scroll, and to open its seals; for You were slain, and have redeemed us to God by Your blood out of every tribe and tongue and people and nation, and have made us kings and priests to our God; and we shall reign on the earth"* (Revelation 5:9-10).

Do you see how worship and intercessory prayer release prophetic songs and words and actions? Undoubtedly, this is what has been happening across the world in the past couple of decades as the prayer and worship movement has swept the Church. The phrase *harp and bowl* has become well-known. Day-and-night prayer, which has been stirred up in multiple locations, is emulating the prayer in Heaven. It is global and transcultural. Believers do not have to be experts to do it. Everybody can be involved. Just as it is in Heaven, so it is on Earth; prayer and worship enhance each other, complement and ignite each other, and out of that interaction comes the prophetic flow.

In John's revelation, the Lamb began to read some of the judgments. They were extreme. This was the final word on what is going to happen in Heaven and on the Earth. After the scroll had been completely unrolled and all of the judgments had been uttered, what was the response in Heaven? Again, the loudest prophetic worship imaginable:

> *After these things I heard a loud voice of a great multitude in heaven, saying, "Alleluia! Salvation and glory and honor and power belong to the Lord our God! For true and righteous are His judgments".... And the twenty-four elders and the four living creatures fell down and worshiped God who sat on the throne, saying, "Amen! Alleluia!"...And I heard, as it were, the voice of a great multitude, as the sound of many waters and as the sound of mighty thunderings, saying, "Alleluia! For the Lord God Omnipotent reigns! Let us be glad and rejoice and give Him glory, for the marriage of the Lamb has come, and His wife has made herself ready."*

> *...Then he said to me, "Write: 'Blessed are those who are called to the marriage supper of the Lamb!'" And he said to me, "These are the true sayings of God." And I fell at his feet to worship*

*him. But he said to me, "See that you do not do
that! I am your fellow servant, and of your brethren who have the testimony of Jesus. Worship
God! For the testimony of Jesus is the spirit of
prophecy"* (Revelation 19:1-2, 4, 6-7, 9-10).

This whole time John is writing, remember? We are
reminded when the angel tells him what words to put
down. (*"Write: 'Blessed are those who are called to the
marriage supper of the Lamb!'"*) John must have been in
spiritual shock. By this time, he had been experiencing
ever-increasing levels of revelation for the equivalent of
19 chapters. He had participated in mind-blowing heavenly worship. He had cried out in travailing prayer, and
his prayers had awesome results. Although normally he
certainly would have been able to tell the difference between Jesus and His angels, he was so overcome that
he fell down at the feet of the messenger-angel, only to
be told, "No! Worship God, not me! I am your fellow servant and the servant of those who carry the testimony of
Jesus."

And what is that testimony? The testimony of Jesus is
the spirit of prophecy. That is our testimony too. *"The testimony of Jesus is the spirit of prophecy"* (Rev. 19:10b).

Why do we find ourselves in the midst of so much
prophetic activity when we are worshiping? It is because
that happens to be when we are testifying the best about
the Lord. We are singing His praises and telling of His
goodness. We are using our voices and our gestures and
our minds and our hearts. In the midst of worship, we find
liberty and faith. Often, even if we do not consider ourselves gifted prophets, we partake of the spirit of prophecy. The bottom line is this: *the environment of worship is
conducive to the spirit of prophecy.*

Ideally—and this is why Paul had to spend so much
time on it with the Corinthians—we should have so much

revelation streaming into our midst that we need help regulating it and even limiting it because everybody is tapping into the flow. When the spirit of prophecy is flowing, people want to praise God, share testimonies, read Scripture, demonstrate God's goodness, speak forth His words, and more.

Elements of Prophetic Worship

Practically speaking, how can we increase the effectiveness of our worship in order to release the prophetic flow? I want to touch on some aspects of prophetic worship.

Prophetic worship involves prophetic *"psalms, hymns, and spiritual songs."* Paul told the church at Ephesus:

> *...Be filled with the Spirit, speaking to one another in psalms and hymns and spiritual songs, singing and making melody in your heart to the Lord, giving thanks always for all things to God the Father in the name of our Lord Jesus Christ* (Ephesians 5:18-20 NKJV).

A *psalm* is Scripture put to music. We already have 150 of them in the Book of Psalms. A *hymn* is not necessarily pure Scripture, but rather a Christian theme put to music. A *spiritual song* is an unrehearsed song that comes forth spontaneously during a time of worship, inspired either by the Holy Spirit or by the singer's own spirit.

A spiritual song can be a musical tribute of praise to God that magnifies Him or it can be a song that arises from the corporate spirit of God's people, like an admonition or a charge or an encouragement. It can also be a prophetic song from the Lord in which He speaks to the people. (Do you think you could ever be comfortable enough to let God sing through you? We are so aware of our humanity and weaknesses that we often hold back, at ease only with singing *to* God, not allowing God to sing *through* us.)

After Mary arrived to visit Elizabeth, who was pregnant with John the Baptist, the Holy Spirit moved both women; and Mary, the expectant mother of Jesus, sang a spontaneous spiritual song of worship:

> *My soul magnifies the Lord,*
> *And my spirit has rejoiced in God my Savior.*
> *For He has regarded the lowly state of His*
> *maidservant;*
> *For behold, henceforth all generations will call*
> *me blessed.*
> *For He who is mighty has done great things*
> *for me,*
> *And holy is His name.*
> *And His mercy is on those who fear Him*
> *From generation to generation.*
> *He has shown strength with His arm;*
> *He has scattered the proud in the imagination of*
> *their hearts.*
> *He has put down the mighty from their thrones,*
> *And exalted the lowly.*
> *He has filled the hungry with good things,*
> *And the rich He has sent away empty.*
> *He has helped His servant Israel,*
> *In remembrance of His mercy,*
> *As He spoke to our fathers,*
> *To Abraham and to his seed forever*
> (Luke 1:46-55 NKJV).

Remember that the testimony of Jesus is the spirit of prophecy. You do not have to be known as a "prophet" to partake of that spirit. You might be a teenage bride or a fisherman or a cashier at the grocery store. You do not have to wait for a church service to express your worship in prophetic song. You can praise the Lord right in your workplace.

Wherever you are under that kind of free anointing, you can magnify the Lord prophetically, and you can prophesy to God's people. You can give prophetic instructions or teaching. As I mentioned earlier we can successfully engage the enemy by prophecy. Some of the most powerful weapons of warfare are musical instruments and hearts on fire.

Selection of Songs

When a worship leader and team devote extra time to praying, listening to God, and rehearsing, they will be more sensitive to the Spirit as they choose worship songs, both in advance of the time of worship and spontaneously when the worshipers are together. As a pastor, I know how it feels to arrive with a couple of equally inspired messages, but without a sense of which one to preach, only to receive confirmation of one of them as one worship song builds on another. Somebody went before the Lord and wrote down a song list that was just as prophetic as it would have been to make the selections while worship was underway. Conversely, I know that the Spirit can shift direction so that the worship team abandons their well-prepared song list in favor of a different flow. Both are elements of prophetic worship as the Spirit leads.

Skilled Musicians

The precedent for wordless musical prophecy goes back at least to the time of David: *"David and the commanders of the army set apart for the service some of the sons of Asaph and of Heman and of Jeduthun, who were to prophesy with lyres, harps and cymbals"* (1 Chron. 25:1).

Not everyone can do this, only those who have been gifted with genuine talent and who have developed their skills as musicians. These are the ones who can play unrehearsed music that has a prophetic anointing on it.

I have been in meetings where worship was going very well and yet when one of the musicians began to play under the inspiration of the Spirit, the momentum surged. By inclining my own spirit, I can discern prophetic themes and know something more about the heart of God. Along with the others, I can respond in a way that gives birth to something new.

The Spirit of Prophecy

It would not be a stretch to say that even when people do not use the terminology I have used in this chapter, they are actually engaging in a global prophetic cry for God to bring revival. The Spirit of God has raised up prophetic worship and intercession hand-in-hand across the world in the past 20 years. Grace has been poured out generously, and people have responded.

While Barbara and I were based in Lindale, Texas, from 1993 to 1996, we hosted five prophetic conferences and several prophetic worship and the arts conferences. It was a special time of an acceleration of the prayer movement, the renewals in Toronto and Pensacola, as well as global increase in the prophetic. It was during this time that Paul Baloche, who was the worship leader at our church, wrote the song "Open the Eyes of My Heart." Little did our dear friend Paul or any of us realize where that song would go and what it would cause people to do. It has been covered by dozens of well-known recording artists, translated into many languages worldwide. The result is awe-inspiring. Globally, 24 hours a day, the Body of Christ in unison is crying out to God for the spirit of revelation. It is always special for Barbara and I when we've been overseas to see the words projected and the voices of those celebrating with this song in prophetic worship and intercession. We personally cherish this, but even more I hope you are more stoked than ever to be released in prophetic worship.

Their response moves Heaven, just as we saw with the incense of the prayers of the saints in the Book of Revelation. The people who have composed the music of our day have supplied fresh words of intercession that can be repeated and multiplied 24/7 across the face of the Earth. Some of our greatest accomplishments in spiritual warfare are coming through joyful singing and sincere celebration of the power of the King and the Kingdom of God.

A Sending Prayer

Spirit of Revelation, we address our worship to the One who sits on the throne. Fill us to overflowing with the music of Heaven. By the all-powerful authority of the Lord, release into our spirits the words and melodies that will turn into prophetic declarations of joy.

May our voices become like skillfully played musical instruments in Your masterpiece of worship. Because the testimony of Jesus is the spirit of prophecy, may we who belong to Him repeat the same words of truth that come from the mouths of His worshipers in Heaven. *"Worthy is the Lamb.... To Him who sits on the throne, and to the Lamb, be blessing and honor and glory and dominion forever and ever"* (Rev. 5:12-13). Amen and amen.

Chapter 9

Sharpening Your Prophetic Senses

I believe that the whole Church is supposed to be prophetic, but I am not saying that every person is supposed to be called a "prophet." Many people who are not prophets nevertheless exercise extraordinary gifts of revelation. Ordinary moms and dads and business people have prophetic dreams that are accurate, and they hear God speaking in their daily lives.

Some time ago my prophetic team received a word that the prophetic anointing was going to come so strongly on the Church that it would be hard to tell who the prophets were, and I believe that has happened. No matter what country I visit, it has happened.

But the prophetic anointing is not isolated to a group of prophets. Nobody owns it. It is everywhere.

Laying Hold of the Prophetic Anointing

Each one of us can lay hold of the prophetic anointing, and that prophetic anointing can increase as we

function under it. Each one of us can increase in our prophetic perception.

We can grow in our sensitivity to the movements of
the Spirit, which are, for the most part, invisible. The fact
that we cannot perceive them does not negate them. In
the spiritual realm, something is moving all the time. If
only our senses were not so dull, we would perceive a lot
more.

God is speaking all the time, but most of the time we
do not hear or perceive a thing. If you could be a fly on
the wall of the war room of the enemy, you might hear
strategy like this: "OK, we can't stop God from speaking. But do everything you can to stop people from hearing Him. Do anything to prevent God's word from bearing
fruit. Get people worried about their money. Get them
interested in sports and fashions. Get them listening to
voices that have nothing to do with the living and active
word of God."

Something inside us should react to that! What has
been distracting us from hearing God's voice? We do not
have to fall for that tactic.

As a first step to sharpening our prophetic sensitivity, all we have to do is *want* it. We need to desire to
prophesy (remember First Corinthians 14:1,39), and we
need to aspire to become more sensitive to God's voice.

Remember that you have an organ of perception—
your own spirit. I mentioned the Greek word *aistheterion*
in Chapter 7, which is translated as "senses" in Hebrews
5:14—*"Solid food is for the mature, who because of practice have their senses trained to discern good and evil."* In
that verse, discernment is portrayed as the direct result
of practice.

Just before that verse, the writer of Hebrews had be-
moaned the condition of the Church:

...You have become dull of hearing. For though by this time you ought to be teachers, you need someone to teach you again the first principles of the oracles of God; and you have come to need milk and not solid food. For everyone who partakes only of milk is unskilled in the word of righteousness, for he is a babe (Hebrews 5:11-13 NKJV).

The Hebrew Christians, like so many of us, needed to be hand-fed even the most elementary things. Like us they had been believers for quite some time, so they should have matured by that time. They could not handle very much revelation because they had not worked up to it.

Why do some people zoom into all sorts of things as soon as they become believers while others just fade into the wallpaper? The difference lies in their desire and the resulting effort. Those people are excited about God, and they want to know everything He will show them. They hunger to learn about Him, and they are not afraid to try new things. They step out in faith all the time, which means that they get lots of practice. Each time they step out in faith, they get a little more light. They are intentional about it, and their actions build on each other like spiritual exercises.

Fifteen times in the Gospels and in the Book of Revelation, Jesus says, *"He who has ears to hear, let him hear"* (see, for example, Luke 14:35). He recognized that people had the right equipment to hear with, but that not everyone was getting it. He was urging people to sharpen their spiritual perception.

He Who Has Ears to Hear, Let Him Hear

One of the times Jesus said, *"He who has ears to hear, let him hear,"* was when He told the parable of the sower (see Mark 4:3-23; see also Luke 8:5-15). Most people believe that this parable is about evangelism, but it is not. It is about hearing and obeying the words of God.

When Jesus opened His mouth to begin telling this story, He hinted at what He was about to say when He said, *"Listen to this!"* (Mark 4:3). In the King James Version, the word is *"Hearken!"* Then He went on to tell the story about how the sower cast his seeds and how some of them were eaten by the birds, some of them sprung up too quickly and then were scorched by the sun, some of them were choked out by thorns and thistles, and only some of them grew well and matured so the plants could bear fruit.

Then when He explained the parable to His disciples, He made it clear that understanding this parable was fundamental to understanding others and that the seeds represented the words of God. *"Do you not understand this parable? How will you understand all the parables? The sower sows the word"* (Mark 4:13-14).

The parable portrays the various responses to hearing and receiving the words of God. It concerns learning to hear the words of God and applying them so that they can bear abundant fruit, *"thirty, sixty, and a hundredfold"* (Mark 4:8,20). The parable is about having ears to hear and the spiritual perception to discern what is going on instead of allowing the words to be (1) snatched away by doubt, unbelief, or fear, (2) withered away by distractions, pressure, or hardship, or (3) choked out by thorns and thistles such as the deceitfulness of riches or the cares of the world. The parable is about letting the words of God grow into mature, fruit-bearing plants, and this does not happen overnight.

God does not distribute and sow His words to excite people or even to build people's faith or enlighten them. He speaks His words so that people will listen and obey them—and allow them to go on to fulfill their purpose of

bearing fruit. Jesus' parable has to do with spiritual perception and hearing the word of God.

Listening for the Voice of the Lord

So the first step to sharpening your prophetic senses
is simply to want to hear. You decide you want to pay
attention. You determine that your efforts will be worth
something because you will meet with God's strong desire
to communicate with you.

The second key to sharpening your prophetic senses
is *awareness*, tuning in. The biblical language is "incline
your ear." You learn to pay attention with your flesh and
blood ears as well as your spiritual ears. This can happen
all the time.

When I am talking with someone, I am listening and
conversing, and at the same time, I have my spiritual an-
tennae up to hear what the Spirit may be saying. God's
voice can be fleeting. He may shift something in my heart
or flash a little picture across my mind in a millisecond. I
have had to practice in order to sharpen my awareness.

Sometimes I have learned the most through the times
when I missed it. When later I could see a confirmation
of the slight sense I had about something, I have learned
what to look for the next time. Of course God will give me
more chances. He knew I would miss it, and He knows
that I will even chicken out sometimes. He allows me to
make progress in baby steps. He will never punish me for
trying.

Besides learning from mistakes, sharpening our prophetic senses takes practice just as any kind of training
involves skill-building repetition. Strengthening spiritual
muscles requires repeated spiritual exercises. To exercise
spiritual muscles, we must repeatedly step out in faith.

Paradoxically, active stepping out in faith involves *resting*—in faith:

> *Therefore, let us fear if, while a promise remains of entering His rest, any one of you may seem to have come short of it....*

> *For we who have believed enter that rest....For He has said somewhere concerning the seventh day: "And God rested on the seventh day from all His works."*

> *...So there remains a Sabbath rest for the people of God. For the one who has entered His rest has himself also rested from his works, as God did from His. Therefore let us be diligent to enter that rest, so that no one will fall, through following the same example of disobedience....*

> *Therefore let us draw near with confidence to the throne of grace, so that we may receive mercy and find grace to help in time of need* (Hebrews 4:1, 3-4,9-11,16).

Most of us, far from resting in faith, exhaust ourselves doing way too much on our own strength. All the while, God wants to tell us what to do and then to help us do it. Life is a whole lot easier that way. All we have to do is listen to Him and then follow through. Step by step by step we follow our Shepherd. We obey supernatural directions by means of His supernatural strength.

Every single ordinary step of faith is significant because it gives a person practice and confidence. When you anticipate worshiping at church because you expect God to speak to you in some way, you are taking a step of faith. When you get there, if you participate in the worship, raising your hands, paying attention to the words, believing the truth, you are following through. The resulting sense of peace or joy, not to mention any particular words that impressed themselves on you, indicate that you have participated in something prophetic and that you have been prophetically sensitive.

You have exercised faith that when the saints are worshiping, you will be able to experience God. In that environment of faith, you have put into practice your faith that God inhabits the praises of His people (see Ps. 22:3). As a result, did your faith increase a bit more? On top of that, did He show you something special? Did you have something to share with others?

This is good news. Listening to God and growing in spiritual perception can be as easy as going to church. In the same way you can perceive the presence of God in worship, you can also sharpen your perception to hear the voice of the Lord at other times.

Flying Practice

I am not Spiritual Superman all the time. Nobody is. But the only way to get off the ground is to practice. Even after "flying" a time or two, we need to stay in shape spiritually by practicing what we preach.

Listen for God's voice all the time. Relax in His company. Become aware of His presence with you during your daily activities. By staying open to the possibility that He might speak to you, you will hear Him when He does. Often His voice is gentle, even casual. The thought may cross your mind, "Today is garbage day." Sometimes it is not just your memory; your Shepherd was helping you stay on top of things.

He is more aware of all the little things you need to do than you are. He is God, and He made you so that He could interact with you. He has the capacity to be involved in the minutiae of your life, as well as with every person in the world, all at the same time, without making anybody come up short. He likes it when we let Him steer.

As often as we let Him direct us, we are sharpening our prophetic senses. Of course we will get it wrong sometimes, but every time we will learn something. As we get better at obeying Him in the small things, He will be able to trust us with bigger things.

I believe in prophetic evangelism. I love setups. Following the Holy Spirit daily into situations that He has set up is a lot easier than presenting the Four Spiritual Laws to somebody on the street. I love it when He directs me to an open parking space, and the next thing I know, I am in the middle of a divine appointment with somebody.

We cannot learn a set of techniques for this. We learn to follow His voice not by following a manual, but rather (what a concept!) by following Emmanuel, God with us.

Obeying the Voice

Why were the Israelites not able to enter God's rest? (See Hebrews 3:11.) It was because they did not obey the voice of the Lord: *"To whom did He swear that they would not enter His rest, but to those who were disobedient? So we see that they were not able to enter because of unbelief"* (Heb. 3:18-19).

If you stop and think about it, the Israelites had a pretty good gig. No wonder they chose not to obey the Voice. They had sandals that would not wear out and free food every day. Living for the moment, they were not particularly interested in facing the giants that were reputed to occupy the Promised Land.

The writer of the letter to the Hebrews quoted a lot from the account of Moses and the people of Israel because it was instructive to people in the Church. Over and over he quoted that one line, *"Today if you hear His voice, do not harden your hearts"* (Heb. 3:8,15; 4:7), which is quoted from a psalm:

> *For He is our God, and we are the people of His pasture and the sheep of His hand. Today, if you would hear His voice, do not harden your hearts, as at Meribah, as in the day of Massah in the wilderness* (Psalm 95:7-8).

He did not want the recipients of his letter to make the same mistake as their predecessors. He wanted them to be able to follow God's voice, obey, and enter God's rest.

Anyone who hardens his or her heart cannot obey God, even after having heard His voice of direction. Hardening your heart is the same as quenching the Spirit. Quenching the Spirit involves refusing to do something you have been told to do or doing something contrary to what you have been told to do. Sometimes we do it out of fear; sometimes we do it out of rebellion; sometimes we do it out of just plain ignorance. We would do well to get real about what we are doing and why we are doing it. God will be patient with us, but we will not have forever to learn to obey Him.

We can quench the Spirit anyplace, even in a powerful, worship-filled meeting. Once I was a guest in a church. The night before I had a powerful dream, and when I got to the meeting I started seeing a vision that related to my skydiving days. Suddenly during worship it all came together, this revelation that had taken something like 27 years to complete. As a result, the power of God began to be manifested in the meeting and those of us who were ministering began to prophesy and speak from Scripture. Some of the guests just prostrated themselves on the platform, humbly receiving God's word as the Spirit imparted it. Without warning, one of the host pastors burst out laughing. He thought He was responding to the Spirit, but he was not. It broke the atmosphere. No way could we get back to it. I knew that if we had just pressed in a little more, we all would have had some type of a heavenly visitation. I was so disappointed. The Spirit had been quenched.

One of the other guests had a mature response. He considered it a learning experience, and he could handle the laughter with patience. He knew that any of us are just average, even on our best days, and that we are all still learning. So it was OK. I took away from that experience an even greater desire to listen to the Spirit and to obey Him.

We will find freedom and anointing on the other side of practiced obedience. In our church, a woman began to want to respond to the prophetic moves of God. The very first time she felt she got a word from Him that she was supposed to share with the people, she came up to me with one of those little spiral notebooks, about the size of a deck of cards, and she was trembling so hard that she could hardly read what she had written down. It was a simple word, but it was God. It would not have been difficult for many other people to do what she did. But for her, it felt like jumping out of an airplane. After a few years, she gained both confidence and skill at discerning and delivering the word of the Lord. Now whenever she speaks up, she nails it. Her practicing and her risk-taking have paid off.

Another good example of hearing and obeying happened on a ministry trip to France. Before I left home with a team of worship-leaders and a dance team, we decided we wanted to bring a gift with us. We had the idea to make them a banner that said (in French, of course) something like, "Lamb Glorious." My wife and her banner-making friends got to work. (Just an aside: sometimes it drives me a little nuts to have a wife who makes worship banners. The attic in our house is filled with all of this shiny, bright fabric, and bells and whistles and glitter and glue and sequins and golden crowns. The place looks like Santa Claus' workshop....)

Anyway, they made a beautiful banner, and they put it in a box, and we took it with us. Nobody at the French church knew we were bringing this gift. I kept it in the back, intending to present it when I got up to speak. As it turned out, the worship leader had wrestled all night long with choosing the music for worship that day. When I asked him at the beginning of the meeting, he still was not sure about which songs to use. But as worship got underway, they started singing song after song about the Lamb of God! My spiritual thermometer was rising. When I opened the box and presented the banner, the power of God fell on that place. We began to minister prophetically. Everything we said caused new openings of revelatory grace. Our earlier obedience released far more than we had expected, and everything we did sharpened our senses further.

Looking Intently

Every time you pick up something that God is saying, you are sharpening your sensitivity to His voice. Every single time. So it is definitely worth pressing in for more.

When we read in the Bible that Peter or Paul "looked intently" or with a "fixed gaze" at someone, I think they were pressing in for revelation. (See Acts 3:4 and Acts 14:9.) They were trying to perceive what was happening inside the person as well as what the Spirit was doing. As soon as they gained the understanding they were looking for, their faith rose high enough to step into the circumstance with supernatural power. These are examples of the spirit of revelation releasing faith (refer back to Chapter

3, "Revelation and Faith"). Their prophetic senses became sharper as a result.

I was in a church in Minneapolis that had been experiencing sustained renewal. The teenagers were coming to the meetings in large numbers. A 14-year-old boy came up to me, and he was crying. He said, "I think there is a woman here who has something wrong in the veins in her leg, and it's painful, and God wants to heal it." One woman began to cry, and she came forward so the boy could pray for her. But as he started to pray, he said, "No, there is someone else here with varicose veins. Actually, more than one other person. And some women have judged others because they have varicose veins." Suddenly, a large number of women responded, and about 40 of them were healed and delivered from their condition because one teenage boy picked up on the condition of one person and had the courage to stand up and say so. As he focused his attention on the situation, more revelation came.

On a Mission

Regardless of how ordinary you may feel your life is, you are on a mission for God. When you go to church or your home group or you leave your house to do an errand, remember to say, "Lord, I want to stir myself up. I want to hear Your voice, and I want to be able to obey You."

When I was a new pastor, Barbara and I really needed a car, and we did not want to go into debt for it. We were humbled when somebody gave us a brand-new car. Granted, it was a Chevy Vega, which is not a luxury vehicle, but it was just what we needed. Back then, Christians all had bumper stickers. Now that I had a bumper to stick one onto, I found a bumper sticker that I felt suited us perfectly. It said, simply, *On a Mission.*

That bumper sticker ministered to me. Every time I loaded up the car and headed out in it, I would see it, and I would remember: *This is no ordinary day. God is going to speak to me today. God has ordered my steps today.* My prophetic sensitivity would go up along with my expectation.

If we are going to be a prophetic people, we need to remind ourselves to listen to God. Then, after we have heard something, we need to take a step of faith and do whatever it is that we are supposed to do. It will never happen if we're just thinking about it. As you know, it is a lot easier to steer a vehicle that is already moving than one that is parked.

Do not wait to "feel led" to listen and obey. Too many Christians fall for that one, and I think that they are dying of "led poisoning." Just step up to the Master and ask for your marching orders. God has called you on a mission too, and He will lead you. If you are already on your feet, He will be able to tell you where to take your next step of faith. Remember what we find in the Book of Chronicles: *"The eyes of the Lord run to and fro throughout the whole earth, to show Himself strong on behalf of those whose heart is loyal to Him..."* (2 Chron. 16:9 NKJV).

When you risk taking that first step of faith, you will be surprised how much revelation and faith will be added to you. Of course the enemy will try to scorch and wither the word before it has been able to grow. Of course there will be some thorns and thistles growing up to choke it out. Naturally, even supernatural growth will seem slow sometimes. But once you have received a word from God and you have acted on it responsibly, you will receive more. You will step into your role as a prophetic person in the Body of Christ.

Do not get distracted from your mission. Do not get tired of hearing God. Do not be like a prophetic friend of mine who had just finished a long and tiring day at a conference and was walking back to his room to take a break between sessions. As he was walking across the grounds, he was sort of complaining to God, saying, "Lord, I hate it when these people keep coming up at the end of the meeting to ask me for a 'word.'"

The Lord rebuked him, lovingly, on the spot. "You hate it??" He said, "I *love* it." The Spirit of God drew him a mental image of those people, and He said, "A time will come when those people will mature so that they can hear from Me themselves. In the meantime, at least they *want* to hear a word from Me."

Nurture the seeds of the word that have been planted in the soil of your spirit. Help them grow and bear fruit. The world needs the word of the Lord. As Moses told the Israelites, *"...Man shall not live by bread alone; but man lives by every word that proceeds from the mouth of the Lord"* (Deut. 8:3 NKJV).

A Sending Prayer

Thank You, Father, for giving each of us a mission. And thank You for speaking to many of us for years already, although sometimes we did not realize that we were hearing Your voice.

Now we need boldness and perseverance. We need Your help to get moving and to stay moving, always looking for more from Your hand.

We need an activation. We are praying for a renewal of grace for the sharpening of our prophetic senses. We want to obey You, reach the people You will be placing in our way, and fulfill Your plans for our lives. Amen.

Chapter 10
Pilgrimage to Destiny

When I reach the end of my life, I want to be able to have the testimony of Jesus. I want to be able to say to Him, "I did the work You wanted me to do, and I did not do it in my own strength. Even though I was not entirely sure what all of the work was, I know You sent me back when I was a young man so that I could do something, and I tried to follow You so I could do it."

When I almost died more than 40 years ago, I would have preferred to have stayed with Him in Heaven. Once I got there, believe me, I did not want to come back here. Heaven is a far better place than this messed-up Earth. But I came back because I wanted to do whatever He told me to do. I wanted to be able to say with both humility and integrity, "Lord, I received the assignments You gave me to do, and by Your grace I accomplished the work." I came back because I wanted to be able to fulfill His prophetic intention for my life, and I still do. I have not yet completed the journey. But by the time He calls me home, I want to have accomplished my God-given destiny.

Echoing the words of the apostle Paul, I can say: *"I do not consider my life of any account as dear to myself, so that I may finish my course and the ministry which I received from the Lord Jesus, to testify solemnly of the gospel of the grace of God"* (Acts 20:24).

By Faith

Why have I been so eager to surrender to God's will? Why do any of us choose to surrender control over our own precious lives (and of our own volition, too)? We surrender because of His touch. He has touched us with His love. He has persuaded us that we will find our lives by losing them. That is one of His clearest messages, and we can find it stated in so many words throughout the four Gospels (see Matt. 10:39; 16:25; Mark 8:35; Luke 9:24; 17:33; John 12:25).

The Father has claimed us as His own, and He has made it possible for us to complete our destiny by sending His Son to redeem us. We can respond because deep inside we are eager to fulfill the purposes for which He created us. What a joy! While millions of other people turn their backs on Him and, therefore, live lives of futility, we have chosen to respond to Him and, thereby, live lives of satisfaction. In the present, we have Heaven-ordained goals, and we have Heaven as our ultimate destination.

By giving ourselves to Him and surrendering ourselves to His purposes, we have put our faith in the promises of our invisible God who makes Himself plain through His abundant words to us. Peter (who learned firsthand about how much God wanted him to fulfill his destiny) summed it up when he wrote:

Blessed be the God and Father of our Lord Jesus Christ, who according to His great mercy has caused us to be born again to a living hope through the resurrection of Jesus Christ from the dead, to obtain an inheritance which is imperishable and undefiled and will not fade away, reserved in heaven for you, who are protected by the power of God through faith for a salvation ready to be revealed in the last time.

In this you greatly rejoice, even though now for a little while, if necessary, you have been distressed by various trials, so that the proof of your faith, being more precious than gold which is perishable, even though tested by fire, may be found to result in praise and glory and honor at the revelation of Jesus Christ; and though you have not seen Him, you love Him, and though you do not see Him now, but believe in Him, you greatly rejoice with joy inexpressible and full of glory, obtaining as the outcome of your faith the salvation of your souls (1 Peter 1:3-9).

Besides obtaining salvation and even commendation, you and I want the Father to be able to glorify Himself in us. We can insert ourselves into Jesus' high priestly prayer, praying for ourselves and for others: "Lord, I glorified You on the earth, having accomplished the work which You gave me to do. I have manifested Your name to the people whom You gave Me. Father, I desire that they will be with me when I come to You" (see John 17:4,6,24).

The bottom line is that I want to live a fruitful life, and I am sure that you do, too. By the end of my life, I want to have given the Lord my undivided attention for decades so that He will have had more opportunity to bring His Kingdom to the people He wanted to reach through me.

James wrote that God *"jealously desires the Spirit which He has made to dwell in us"* (James 4:5). His Father-heart wants us to recognize that the only *worthwhile* work we can do originates from Him and is executed through Him. He wants us to press on in spite of the potential deterrent of inevitable hardships; He does not want us to miss it.

Prophetic Word and Your Personal Destiny

Have you noticed? Sometimes when God tells us that something is going to occur, the opposite starts to happen. Just as soon as you begin to understand and follow His plan for your life, every weird thing that could go wrong does go wrong.

You know what that is, don't you? It is the devil trying to rob you of the word that God spoke to you. He plays up all of your weaknesses so that you are tripping over yourself when you do the simplest things. He whispers reasonable-sounding things to you that undermine your confidence. He makes every effort to convince you that you are becoming too radical, too extreme, "too prophetic," out of touch with reality, holier-than-thou, whatever....

Because you want to hear God and obey Him, the devil will be tireless in his efforts to thwart your desire. Just as in the parable of the sower, which we explored in the previous chapter, the "seed" of God's words must grow to maturity through many hazards and threats. Much of the time for many of us, the growing conditions prove to be too hostile. The seed of God's word gets snatched by the devil; the barely sprouted seedlings get scorched by the sun; the apparently healthy plants (almost ready to start bearing seed themselves) get choked out by weeds of the worries and cares of life.

Does it have to be this way? I do not think so. You and I are not quite as helpless in the face of our circumstances as seeds are. When God's words are "planted" in our spirits and minds, we can, for one thing, recognize the threats as they arise and ask God for help. We have a choice in the matter. To change the analogy to another biblical one, we can choose *not* to shipwreck our faith (see 1 Tim. 1:18-19). We can choose not to let our human weaknesses derail us.

Wounded Soldiers

Granted, we are all "wounded soldiers." Spiritually and emotionally (often mentally and physically as well), we walk with a limp. The circumstances of life, even after we enter the Kingdom, have been hard on us.

All of us have trusted in ourselves when we should have trusted in God. Ironically, when we trust in ourselves, we feel we are relying on our strengths, although anytime we lean on ourselves more than we lean on Him, really we are choosing to rely on weakness. So often when we operate out of our own weak and wounded selves, we do more damage than good. Sadly, wounded soldiers often continue to rely on their own strength and follow their own "lights," often shipwrecking their destinies in the process. Wounded soldiers find it nearly impossible to fight the good fight of faith consistently (see 1 Tim. 6:12).

Human nature works against us. You know, when God got the children of Israel out of Egypt, He did not want them to have to wander in the desert for 40 years. He wanted them to go straight into the Promised Land. But they would not fight for it. They could not achieve it. They let the enemy rob them. They allowed fears and complacency to rule their hearts. ("The giants are too big! It will be too hard!") They trusted only in what they could figure out for themselves.

The Promised Land is like the promises of God in our lives. Will we fight the good fight of faith, believing that God is bigger than any problem and that nothing is impossible for Him? Or will we wither in the face of the opposition? Will we stand strong, or will we turn tail like even the mighty Elijah did? (Remember the story from First Kings 18–19?) Elijah was a wounded soldier. So was Peter, especially after the crucifixion. (Remember how Jesus had to restore him in John 21?) I believe that Peter had lost his hope of fulfilling his destiny as a disciple of

Jesus and a man of God. He had messed up so badly, denying his Lord who, as far as he knew, he would never see again.

Elijah's and Peter's stories prove one thing that all of us need to hear—God wants us to fulfill our destinies even more than we want to, and He loves us so much that He will intervene to enable us to get back on track. God always makes a way. In impossible-seeming situations, He made sure that they did not shipwreck themselves. The power of Heaven proved to be stronger than their wounded humanity.

Ideally, whenever we see that our humanness is getting in the way of our obedient response to the word of God, we should at least recognize our need for help instead of ignoring the only One who can heal us and help us mature.

Finding Healing for Life's Wounds

God has ordained a destiny for you; He holds a plan and a purpose for your life. You can believe that as a solid fact even as you also recognize the enemy's fingerprints on your shiny, golden Destiny.

The damage is more serious than a mere collection of fingerprints; we have bruises and lacerations and fractures. In fact, putting yourself in the light of His Kingdom positions your scars and wounds in the spotlight. You may have thought some of these things were merely personality traits or basic components of your physical, mental, emotional, and spiritual make-up. Now you are not so sure.

When you came into this world, you encountered problems, and when you and others tried to solve them, you created more problems. Soon, your problems outnumbered your solutions. When you met the Lord, He began to help you deal with some of those things, but you remain wounded in ways that have not yet been healed. Even if you have been walking closely with the Lord for a long time, you are always bumping into new areas of yourself that need help.

We wounded soldiers may find ourselves angry when we intend to be calm. We may hurt other people instead of helping them. We may take the easy way out of conflict. We may try to control others. We may admire all of the people who seem to be able to hear God readily and explain what He is saying with ease. Yet when we open our mouths, somehow both of our feet end up in there.

Have you had parents or good friends or leaders who disappointed you, shattering your ability to trust others? Once upon a time, did you step out in faith, convinced that you had received the word of the Lord, only to fall flat on your face? Are you afraid this may happen again? Is your confidence wobbly? Do you expect to fail? Have you become cynical?

I could go on and on. The fact is, even people in the prophetic ministry, people who are supposed to be reflecting the loving image of God for the benefit of others, are wounded soldiers themselves. It is easy to see why this is the case; none of us has "arrived" quite yet. We can try to pretend that we know it all, but we definitely do not. The prophetic ministry is powerful, and just as fire is powerful, it can be useful or destructive depending on the way it is delivered. In the developmental history of mankind, fire as an energy source is probably the key to modern civilization. But fire out of control is threatening, fearful, wasteful, and destructive.

As a prophetic people, we cannot long afford to misuse the fire of God because of our ailing human nature, but neither do we want to put out His fire. We need to present ourselves to Jesus, the perfect prophet, on a daily basis. We need to be transformed into His image.

He *will* send us healing for our woundedness. As He heals us, He will build us into new men and women. He is setting His house in order. We can squirm out of His grasp like wild runaway toddlers, or we can decide to settle into His lap.

> *Now the Lord is the Spirit, and where the Spirit of the Lord is, there is liberty. But we all, with unveiled face, beholding as in a mirror the glory of the Lord, are being transformed into the same image from glory to glory, just as from the Lord, the Spirit* (2 Corinthians 3:17-18).

Missed Opportunities

I do not know if you can speed God up, but I know you can slow Him down. You can miss opportunities, and you can slow down a process that is already underway. You can take another lap around Mount Sinai in the wilderness before you realize you should have done something differently.

I believe in the sovereignty of God, but I do not believe that He has planned everything that happens to us. Some of our detours and difficulties happen because we are dumb. We are unwise. We bring trouble onto ourselves by failing to obey the word of the Lord. Sometimes, our mistakes and neglect can delay or derail an important part of God's plan for our lives.

Of course God works all things together for good for those who love God and are called according to His purpose (see Rom. 8:28). He is perfectly capable of incorporating our mistakes into His plan. But that does not imply that He foreordains them. We cannot blame Him for our sin; He is not the author of sin. We possess free will.

So when we sin, we have made a wrong choice. We can always avoid sin by our obedience. Just as freely as we can choose to sin, we can choose to obey. Obedience (usually following quick repentance) saves a lot of time and trouble.

Had I obeyed God more often early in my life, I would have avoided some major obstacles. I can't blame Him for not stopping me from missing opportunities or messing up assignments. All I can do is accept those situations, perhaps learn from them, and ask Him to make the best of them.

Even when our circumstances are the direct fulfillment of a prophecy, the way they work out remains conditional upon our response to God's word. Will we use wisdom? Will we pay attention to His voice for the first step only, or will we listen to His direction so we can follow Him all the way?

It is the same for all of us—we can learn the hard way, or we can learn the obedient way. I have learned the hard way too many times. I am tired of learning that way. It is really not fun. How much better it is to do things by obedience and faith!

God will give us a heads-up, sometimes more than once. He loves us. When He sees us wavering, He will bring extra pressure to bear on us. He may send someone else to speak a word of wisdom. He will up the ante in hopes that we will listen. Maybe we will; maybe we won't. You know, you can pay $4.00 now for that new part, or you can pay $1,500.00 later when you blow the engine up.

It pays to keep listening to God!

Step by Step

There is a process between the word of vision and the attainment of destiny. Usually it consists of preparation and equipping and character-building so that you will not end up building your destiny with one hand while tearing it down with the other.

Certainly God wants to make sure that when you get there, you will not be immature and think that you did it by yourself. You need to recognize that you barely made it by the grace of God; He wants to reinforce your trust in Him. Next time you receive a word from Him, He wants you to believe it and confess it in a healthier way, even as you test and judge it and hold onto it as you endure a time of shaking.

The fulfillment of a prophetic word is a process. Through revelation and sharpening your prophetic gifts, living in faith, growing up in God, you will grow more in love, more in faith, more in grace, and more in life. Not only will you learn that *"eye has not seen, nor ear heard, nor have entered into the heart of man the things which God has prepared for those who love Him"* (1 Cor. 2:9 NKJV), but also you will learn that you can only walk those things out by cooperating with the growth process. Not only does God reveal His purposes through His Spirit, but also He reveals the steps. Each step is a new revelation. It is a dynamic process involving one supernatural encounter after another, your responses to God's initiatives and your faith-filled responses to other people and circumstances.

All that being said, sometimes God makes the process very short. Sometimes the fulfillment of prophecy, especially for a young Christian, seems to happen automatically. One time I was involved with a group of people and a little revival broke out. I told them they needed to be water-baptized as well as being filled with the Spirit. So they got together in the backyard of a couple who had a swimming pool. The wife was one of the radicals who had gotten involved with us, but her husband was not.

While we were having our group baptism, her husband came home from work. He thought it was a party. He said, "Well, I would like to get baptized too." I don't think he got saved until he hit the water. All he had said was, "I just want Jesus to help me have a good life."

After he got baptized, something happened. We took him into the house and prayed over him. Somebody got a prophetic word for him, something along the lines of, "God is going to promote you; there is an increase coming in your life."

Now this guy was well-to-do already. He was young, but he had a tremendous job. He had never heard a prophecy before. He said to his wife, "That must refer to the promotion I just got because I could never get another promotion."

A month later, he did get another promotion at work. It should have taken five years of effort before he would even have been considered for it. Then a week later, the company he worked for merged with another one, and he got another promotion by virtue of the merger.

He was blown away. So was I. This guy was already doing well, and now he was doing better. God seemed to want to endorse and underline his salvation, all without sending him through tests and trials. I said to the Lord, "That's not fair. I've had more trials than Perry Mason.... But never mind, You can do whatever You want. If You can convert people with swimming-pool water, You can promote people without putting them through a process."

I am sure that by now God has allowed some kind of trouble into that wealthy guy's life because that is how He does things. Normally we can expect our growth to be a process that involves some challenges. You know as well as I do that the progress is worth it:

Consider it all joy, my brethren, when you encoun-
ter various trials, knowing that the testing of your
faith produces endurance. And let endurance have
its perfect result, so that you may be perfect and
complete, lacking in nothing (James 1:2-4).

Explain what getting grounded mean

Receiving and Responding

In Christ, you and I have become new creatures. Like
seeds planted in good soil, we are destined to grow. God
has a level of mature fruitfulness that He wants us to attain, and He has prepared "good works" for us to perform:
"For we are His workmanship, created in Christ Jesus for
good works, which God prepared beforehand so that we
would walk in them" (Eph. 2:10). We walk into those good
works prophetically, living out His intention and purpose
for our lives.

For young Believer

The first step in the development of a seed (a natural
seed and also the "seed" of the word of God) happens in
the dark, underground where nobody can see any growth.
The seed "dies" to its old existence in favor of the new
one. Unseen changes signal important developments. The
outer shell cracks and falls away as new life swells and
grows. Little root hairs go out and begin to pick up nu-
trients. The growing life finds its way upward toward the
light.

At this early stage, we are getting grounded in whatever God's word declared. Even if a cold winter or a dry
season ensues, the word-seed can wait it out. Like winter
wheat, it will not die off; it will grow rapidly once warm
weather comes. Sometimes the word of God will come to
you, and it will seem like everything freezes up afterward.
Don't worry; it is temporary—unless your heart is like the
hardened soil of the parable of the sower (see Mark 4:5,
16-17; see also Luke 8:6,13).

New Growth

Eventually, a visible blade or shoot breaks thro the surface of the soil. Now other people can begii observe the changes. In terms of prophetic fulfillm᷉ this is when things begin to fit together. People c᷉ into your life and circumstances work together. S᷉ people try to run ahead of God's process, and they up with an Ishmael (see Genesis 16). Other people to allow the process to unfold; it is as if they do receive the benefits of the sunlight or the refresh rain.

For example, say you are involved in music mini᷉ in a church. You are aware that you have a destiny cause of a prophetic word that you have received. But fulfillment seems distant. You are doing the same thi you were doing before—maybe even less than bef᷉ Some of your duties seem boring. Not all of them conc music ministry. Other people in your life are pulling you, asking for your time and energy. You spend mos the week simply earning a living or going to school. "B᷉ you say, "I thought God's word would come to pass. Ma᷉ it isn't going to happen."

Do not be discouraged. You are at the very beginn of a process. Where you are right now is important, e᷉ if all you have is a memory of a word being planted ᷉ a souvenir handful of dirt. Whatever you are obligatec do right now, do it with all your heart. Be faithful, botl terms of being reliable and in terms of being full of fai Walk in faith. Every step of faith takes you another s closer to your destiny.

Do not be impatient. Resist the temptation to be l the people who attempt an end run around the preseni order to arrive at the future. Try not to take matters i᷉ your own hands. Enjoy the process and appreciate it. low God to teach you how to walk one step at a time bef᷉ you try to run a marathon. Follow Him step-by-step so that the enemy will not be able to rob you of your hope.

Confidence

As you cooperate with the process, your confidence will grow. You will begin to be able to say, "Yes, I can see growth. I can see God working in my life. I'm becoming equipped; I'm learning things. This is in line with what I believe has been spoken about me prophetically. This must be part of the process. So I rejoice. I thank You, Lord. I know I am taking steps with You. By faith, I believe that I will become more fruitful than this, and yet I can rejoice in what I am doing now."

Learn to enjoy Him on a daily basis. To enjoy Him today, you do not have to know where you will be in a year. By next year this time, the only thing you can be sure of is that you will be in the Spirit—assuming that is the desire of your heart. It does not really matter if your current occupation is unsatisfying or your relationships are confusing. God will carve a way for you in the wilderness. Take the next step with more confidence than you took the last one. Expect your growing process to move forward.

Cultivation

As you proceed toward the fulfillment of God's word to you, He is going to fill you up, feed you, and equip you. In other words, the Master Gardener is going to cultivate you. He will pull out the weeds that threaten to choke your growth. He will nourish you. He will make sure that you get plenty of sunshine.

As you grow into your destiny, you will feel like a young adolescent boy sometimes—all gangly arms and legs, tripping over your feet. But God will supply you with the wisdom and anointing you need to act in faith, and He will present you with plenty of challenges so that you will be able to experiment with your gifts and learn how to tune in to Him prophetically. The goal is to become mature, to grow:

> *...To the measure of the stature which belongs to the fullness of Christ....to grow up in all aspects into Him who is the head, even Christ, from whom the whole body, being fitted and held together by what every joint supplies, according to the proper working of each individual part, causes the growth of the body for the building up of itself in love* (Ephesians 4:13, 15-16).

Do not fret when your growth does not yet seem to match your calling. This is a process, remember. The whole time you will be testing your wings, taking longer and longer flights, doing exploits for Jesus under His anointing as He supplies it. You will be cultivating your gifts and maturing in your call.

I have known people who taught the Bible for 20 or 30 years before they arrived at a destination of real effectiveness. The whole time they were serving God, being anointed, growing. After all those years, suddenly a breakthrough brought them into fullness. They were effective all along, but apparently they were still practicing. I have seen the same process with people who prophesy or pray for healing. Always followers, always learners, they kept at it, increasing in effectiveness and in their level of anointing. Maturing and trusting in the Living Word faithfully, they keep holding the testimony of Jesus until the end of their earthly lives.

They weren't fast-trackers, but that is OK. (You know the kind I mean by "fast-trackers," the ones who just met Jesus six months ago and now they are theological experts. They have their three favorite Scriptures, and they think they know all there is to know about being a Christian.) They were not self-proclaimed "wise guys." Instead, expecting the unexpected on a daily basis, they just kept listening to the Lord and following His advice.

In case you did not realize it, you will never know all there is to know about being a Christian, not on this side of glory anyway. The mind of Christ is as vast as the universe. Job, after all his trials, declared to the Lord,

> I know that You can do anything, and no one can stop You. You asked, "Who is this that questions My wisdom with such ignorance?" It is I—and I was talking about things I knew nothing about, things far too wonderful for me. You said, "Listen and I will speak! I have some questions for you, and you must answer them." I had only heard about You before, but now I have seen you with my own eyes. I take back everything I said, and I sit in dust and ashes to show my repentance (Job 42:2-6 NLT).

Job thought he knew God well, but he discovered that he was wrong. He had his definitions and principles down, but he did not know that God was not obligated to play by his (Job's) rules. God turned out to be bigger, better, and more awesome than anyone realized.

Fruition

In due time, if you are patient, you will arrive at your destiny. God is faithful to complete what He begins. He is the author of your faith and the One who perfects it over time (see Heb. 12:2). He will bring you to the point of being able to operate in your full capacity, motivated by His love, filled with His Spirit.

For your part, you will simply know that He's the One who did it, not you. He supplied the seed and provided the growth *"He who supplies seed to the sower and bread for food will also supply and increase your store of seed and will enlarge the harvest of your righteousness"* (2 Cor. 9:10 NIV). Certainly each step required bigger faith, but that means you are all the more humbly aware that *He* is the Lord of the harvest.

When you really get into the fruit-bearing stage, you will be simple, unpretentious, unpresumptuous—and wiser than ever. And you will be able to stay that way without struggling. What an honor to serve the Lord of the universe, allowing the power of God to come through your earthly vessel, radiating His glory.

All the Way to Zion

Day in and day out, we *"press on toward the goal for the prize of the upward call of God in Christ Jesus"* (Phil. 3:14). We desire to do whatever He tells us to do (see John 2:5). Because He has a path marked out for us, we know that we need His guidance all the way or we will not arrive at our destination.

Each path seems to include detours and rough spots. No one seems to be allowed to travel in first class. It can seem like a slow slog sometimes. But *the path leads to destiny,* and it grows brighter as time goes by. And *"the path of the righteous is like the light of dawn, that shines brighter and brighter until the full day"* (Prov. 4:18).

Alongside His fresh revelations, God's sure promises apply to every one of us as we accept everything from parched desert times to rich, fruitful rewards:

The desert and the parched land will be glad;
the wilderness will rejoice and blossom.

Like the crocus, it will burst into bloom;
it will rejoice greatly and shout for joy.
The glory of Lebanon will be given to it,
the splendor of Carmel and Sharon;
they will see the glory of the Lord,
the splendor of our God.

Strengthen the feeble hands,
steady the knees that give way;

say to those with fearful hearts,
"Be strong, do not fear;
your God will come,
He will come with vengeance;
with divine retribution
He will come to save you."

Then will the eyes of the blind be opened
and the ears of the deaf unstopped.

Then will the lame leap like a deer,
and the mute tongue shout for joy.
Water will gush forth in the wilderness
and streams in the desert.

The burning sand will become a pool,
the thirsty ground bubbling springs.
In the haunts where jackals once lay,
grass and reeds and papyrus will grow.

And a highway will be there;
it will be called the Way of Holiness.
The unclean will not journey on it;
it will be for those who walk in that Way;
wicked fools will not go about on it.

No lion will be there,
nor will any ferocious beast get up on it;
they will not be found there.
But only the redeemed will walk there,

and the ransomed of the Lord will return.
They will enter Zion with singing;
everlasting joy will crown their heads.
Gladness and joy will overtake them,
and sorrow and sighing will flee away
(Isaiah 35 NIV).

A Sending Prayer

Father in Heaven, we want to receive with both hands the gifts, the callings, and the destinies You have set before each one of us. We pray for Your continuous help and Your ongoing anointing. We ask always for more wisdom, growing maturity, and fresh mercies. Without the power of Your Spirit, we have no ability to live lives that bring honor to You, that glorify You, that produce fruit, and that bring us into the destiny that You have set before us.

Thank You for teaching us how to walk in faith. Thank You for the atmosphere of faith that we have experienced in the Body of Christ. We are grateful for Your grace, and we want to walk in it always. In Jesus' name, amen.

Chapter 11

The Word Made Sure

The Word of God is filled with promises. If you never received a single direct prophetic word from the Lord, His promises in the Bible are God-breathed invitations for Kingdom realities. In both the Old Testament and the New, He declares, "I will be with you. I will strengthen you. I will be all that you need. I will provide for you." We should never grow tired of reviewing and living by faith in the promises contained in His written Word.

And yet the written Word is *not* enough. God Himself says so within its pages, where He urges His people to seek His face continually, to listen to Him, to be ready to hear and obey fresh words from Heaven (see, for example, 1 Chron. 16:11; Ps. 27:4; Isa. 26:9; Col. 3:1, and more). Those fresh words, whether whispered by the Spirit into our own hearts or broadcasted loudly by a prophetic preacher, are like manna to our spirits. To understand and receive His invitations we need the Holy Spirit. It takes revelation, interpretation, and application.

When it is an authentic word from Heaven, a brand-new prophetic word nourishes our spirits because it lines up perfectly with God's scriptural promises. The promises in the Bible represent the favorite themes of the Holy Spirit, and He wants us to know them by heart.

What themes and promises should we be on the look-out for? Here are a dozen of the most important ones.

Eternal Life

This is the biggie, the one that even nonbelievers know about. Like all of God's promises, it is conditional. To put in your reservation for a seat in Heaven, you need to *"believe in the Lord Jesus, and you will be saved"* (Acts 16:31) because *"there is salvation in no one else; for there is no other name under heaven that has been given among men by which we must be saved"* (Acts 4:12).

Eternal life (which starts now, before you die) is your biggest reward for being "born again" or "saved." You have been saved from a life of futility on earth and from an eternity of death after death. You have been saved for a life that grows richer and more abundant while you remain on earth and for a future of unspeakable delight after you die, when God brings your spirit to live with Him in Heaven.

Righteousness, Peace, and Joy in the Holy Spirit

As a born-again, pre-qualified citizen of Heaven, you have been granted an inheritance that cannot be taken away. As a citizen of God's Kingdom (see Matthew 6:10, *"...on earth as it is in Heaven"*), you have been promised imperishable righteousness, peace, and joy.

These are not only promises, but also present realities, renewable daily because of the abiding presence of the Holy Spirit. *"The kingdom of God is...righteousness and peace and joy in the Holy Spirit"* (Rom. 14:17).

Blessed be the Lord God of Israel,
For He has visited us and accomplished redemp-
tion for His people,

And has raised up a horn of salvation for us
In the house of David His servant—

As He spoke by the mouth of His holy prophets
from of old—

Salvation from our enemies,
And from the hand of all who hate us;

To show mercy toward our fathers,
And to remember His holy covenant,

The oath which He swore to Abraham our father,

To grant us that we, being rescued from the
hand of our enemies,
Might serve Him without fear,

In holiness and righteousness before Him all our
days (Luke 1:68-75).

Filled with His Spirit of righteous holiness, we are better equipped all the time to minister peace and joy to others in Jesus' name.

Justification, Sanctification, Glorification

These are big, theological-sounding words for parts of the overall promise of eternal, abundant life. In fact, these three terms are like the three "verb tenses" of salvation: Past (justification: see Ephesians 2:8), Present (sanctification: see Philippians 2:12), and Future (glorification: see Romans 13:11).

Justification is the spiritual regeneration that happens when we exchange our old selves for new ones (see Rom. 6:4). Sanctification is our ongoing salvation as we live and grow in grace and holiness. Part of sanctification is the process of healing and maturation that we discussed in the previous chapter and in Chapter 4. The goal is glorification, being like Him. God's Spirit will shepherd each one of us through the process. Here's a promise for you: *"...He who began a good work in you will perfect it until the day of Christ Jesus"* (Phil. 1:6).

Glorification happens when you arrive in "Glory," as the old-timers used to call Heaven.

> *Beloved, now we are children of God, and it has not appeared as yet what we will be. We know that when He appears, we will be like Him, because we will see Him just as He is. And everyone who has this hope fixed on Him purifies himself, just as He is pure* (1 John 3:2-3).

Glorification also happens before we get to Heaven. It happens every time God's loving, powerful presence shines forth from His people. The people *"...whom He called, He also justified; and these whom He justified, He also glorified"* (Rom. 8:30).

Because you have been justified and you are being sanctified, you can expect the glory of God to shine through you. This is not an ego trip; it is a glory trip. And it is a visible evidence of the reality of God. You can try to explain Him to other people, but when they see Him in, on, and through you, your countenance will witness to Him better than any words you can put together.

His Eternal Presence

The Father promised that His Holy Spirit would be with you forever. Jesus said:

I will ask the Father, and He will give you another Helper, that He may be with you forever; that is the Spirit of truth, whom the world cannot receive, because it does not see Him or know Him, but you know Him because He abides with you and will be in you (John 14:16-17).

The Holy Spirit does not come and go. He dwells in you permanently. Although you can suppress your awareness of His still, small voice, you can also stir yourself up to listen to Him in prayer. You can allow His presence to saturate you in glory, like a foretaste of Heaven.

His eternal presence with you is that *"river of living water"* that Jesus talked about: *"He who believes in Me, as the Scripture said, 'From his innermost being will flow rivers of living water'"* (John 7:38; see also John 4:14). The Spirit is like an artesian well, an inexhaustible supply. With His presence you have fullness of joy—and a bubbling up of prophetic words (see Ps. 16:11). Jesus promised, *"I am with you always, even to the end of the age"* (Matt. 28:20).

Gifts and "Greater Works"

One sunny day, Jesus prophesied to the people who were listening to Him, *"Truly, truly, I say to you, he who believes in Me, the works that I do, he will do also; and greater works than these he will do; because I go to the Father"* (John 14:12).

I used to struggle with that one. How could such a thing be true? Jesus healed the blind and raised the dead. How could someone like me do greater works than those? Sure, He never prayed for a new car or a hundred dollars—because they weren't invented yet in the first century—but I know that is not what He was talking about.

I have a friend who is fiery and bold. When he came to the Lord, he began to pray to the Lord every day to be able to receive every single gift of the Spirit, every promise, everything he could possibly get. By now, he has manifested every gift of the Holy Spirit at least once in his life because he wanted to do it so badly.

What if I wanted badly enough to do *"greater works"* than Jesus? What if I didn't delineate any boundaries for the Holy Spirit (telling Him, "Lord, You can ask me to do so and so, but I will never do such and such.")? What if I kept listening to the Spirit so I would know what works He wants to do today and every day?

Power to Witness

Here is another promise, straight from the lips of Jesus one minute before He ascended into Heaven: *"You shall receive power when the Holy Spirit has come upon you; and you shall be witnesses to Me in Jerusalem, and in all Judea and Samaria, and to the end of the earth"* (Acts 1:8).

He might have also added, "You shall have supernatural boldness in the face of fear," because when you go out in the power of the Spirit, you will be heading into enemy territory. People will not always welcome your witness. Sure, the Gospel is *"the power of God for salvation to everyone who believes..."* (Rom. 1:16), but that is only if you can overcome your fears fully, or at least enough to open your mouth.

I think it is interesting that whenever an angel shows up (or Jesus, after His resurrection), the first thing he has to say is, "Fear not," "Don't be afraid." The holiness of God is awesome. The power of His presence, even when mitigated by an angel or another one of His servants, can make you quake in your sandals. His power is supernatural, and it makes things happen that could not happen by any natural power.

Provision (With Persecution)

Oh, yes, God has promised to give us every single thing we will ever need—along with a hefty dose of hardship and persecution:

> *Jesus said, "Truly I say to you, there is no one who has left house or brothers or sisters or mother or father or children or farms, for My sake and for the gospel's sake, but that he will receive a hundred times as much now in the present age, houses and brothers and sisters and mothers and children and farms, along with persecutions; and in the age to come, eternal life* (Mark 10:29-30).

Not many of us have underlined that one in our Bibles, have we? "Oh boy, persecutions; bring 'em on!" Not me. Of course, not many of us have left everything behind for the sake of the Gospel either, so maybe we won't have to worry about the resultant heavy persecution—nor will we have much fruit to show for our sacrifices.

All of us have left things behind, though, and all of us have experienced God's compensation system, at least to a degree. And you have found it to be true that whenever you have followed Him, He has taken care of you. Whatever you have left behind, He has made up to you more than you expected. The persecution part may not have seemed as significant to you as you thought it would. Most of us have endured some level of persecution, even if it was only a funny look or being rejected somehow.

Blessing

Peter wrote this promise down: *"...You were called for the very purpose that you might inherit a blessing"* (1 Pet. 3:9). God did not call you so that you could inherit calamity or disaster or disappointment or failure. He called you so that you would be in a position to receive His blessing.

Here again, His blessing is a "mixed blessing," although ultimately the outcome is pure joy. In His sermon on the mount, Jesus put it this way:

> *Blessed are those who have been persecuted for the sake of righteousness, for theirs is the kingdom of heaven. Blessed are you when people insult you and persecute you, and falsely say all kinds of evil against you because of Me. Rejoice and be glad, for your reward in heaven is great; for in the same way they persecuted the prophets who were before you* (Matthew 5:10-12).

Jesus' close friend, John the apostle, affirmed the promises of blessings when he said, *"From the fullness of His grace we have all received one blessing after another"* (John 1:16 NIV).

Redemption of the Body

Most of us never really think about this one. The promises in the Bible are pretty definite: When we see Him, we are going to be like Him:

> *Our citizenship is in heaven. And we eagerly await a Savior from there, the Lord Jesus Christ, who, by the power that enables Him to bring everything under His control, will transform our*

lowly bodies so that they will be like His glorious body (Philippians 3:20-21 NIV).

We are already God's children, but He has not yet shown us what we will be like when Christ appears. But we do know that we will be like Him, for we will see Him as He really is (1 John 3:2 NLT).

That means you and I are going to have resurrected bodies because He does. No matter how health-conscious you have been, you are going to be a whole lot healthier in the translation to your heavenly body. I'm looking forward to this one: I am going to get to live forever in a body that does not show evidence of aging and wear and tear, not to mention a certain horrific accident.

Fellowship With Him and His Saints

Another guarantee in the written Word is fellowship—companionship, enjoyment, company—with the Father and Jesus through the Spirit and with fellow believers. This is another promise that applies to every believer:

God is faithful, through whom you were called into fellowship with His Son, Jesus Christ our Lord (1 Corinthians 1:9).

What we have seen and heard we proclaim to you also, so that you too may have fellowship with us; and indeed our fellowship is with the Father, and with His Son Jesus Christ (1 John 1:3).

If we walk in the Light as He Himself is in the Light, we have fellowship with one another... (1 John 1:7).

As with other promises, this promised fellowship is conditional upon our receptivity. Will we walk in His light?

Will we allow "fellowship" to become an active verb that will characterize our lives? We can have it if we want it.

Rewards

Jesus indicated that, according to how well we have followed His Spirit, doing what He tells us to do, there will be benefits: *"The Son of Man will come in the glory of His Father with His angels, and then He will reward each according to his works"* (Matt. 16:27 NKJV).

Throughout the Bible, you can find more evidence that He is generous almost to a fault. Think of the story of the prodigal son (see Luke 15). Most of us think that *prodigal* means something bad, but that is not what the word means; it simply means he was a big spender. The story could have been titled the Parable of the Prodigal Father because in the end, the father out-spent his wayward son, generously welcoming him back in spite of what he had done. The young man's father lavished love and affection on him as well as giving him food and clothing and a princely welcome back to the home he had repudiated.

Like the father of the prodigal son, God is lavish with His affection and provision. He always goes farther than you think He will. And yet it is not automatic. He is not a name-it-and-claim-it Father. God commends and rewards those who are obedient to Him, especially those who obey in minor things as well as major ones and those who endure hardship in the process. Obedience implies a master-servant or a parent-child relationship. His promises apply to those who walk with Him by faith: *"Without faith it is impossible to please Him, for he who comes to God must believe that He is, and that He is a rewarder of those who seek Him"* (Heb. 11:6).

As I mentioned at the beginning of this chapter, God's desire is recorded in His written word, where He urges people never to stop seeking to hear His voice, individually and corporately:

> **Seek** *the Lord and His strength;* **seek** *His face continually* (1 Chronicles 16:11).

> *One thing I ask of the Lord, this is what I* **seek:** *that I may dwell in the house of the Lord all the days of my life, to gaze upon the beauty of the Lord and to* **seek** *Him in His temple* (Psalm 27:4 NIV).

> *At night my soul longs for You, indeed, my spirit within me* **seeks** *You diligently; for when the earth experiences Your judgments the inhabitants of the world learn righteousness* (Isaiah 26:9).

> *Therefore if you have been raised up with Christ,* **keep seeking** *the things above, where Christ is, seated at the right hand of God* (Colossians 3:1).

As part of the prophetic Church, we can hear His voice for ourselves. Seeking Him guarantees results. We can hear His voice even though we cannot see Him. This is a reward in itself, and yet the day will come when we will be further rewarded simply for having been attentive to Him. The day will come when we will see Him face-to-face. Overwhelmed with joy, we will say, *"I have heard of You by the hearing of the ear; but now my eye sees You"* (Job 42:5).

In this book I did not elaborate on the office of the prophet, the gift of prophecy, prophetic preaching, prophetic intercession, the phenomenon of the prophetic, divine appointments, or prophetic evangelism. We have taught, equipped, and activated extensively on these ministries, and we encourage you to go after these things. However, the intent of this work is to encourage all of God's people to surge forward in the spirit of revelation—believe and expect it!

Also, I've included a good portion of Scripture. It has been my experience when I have listened to solid, anointed teachers that my revelatory gifting starts to spike. In the manner in which we encourage you to grow in the prophetic ministry experientially, we ought to continue to experience God in His Word. *"...Now made manifest, and by the prophetic Scriptures made known to all nations, according to the commandment of the everlasting God, for obedience to the faith"* (Rom. 16:26 NKJV).

Finishing Well

Just after the beginning of the year 2007, I had a very powerful present-truth encounter with God that was both tender and terribly holy.

I had received an e-mail from a member of a church with which I have had a very close relationship for 30 years. It was about the pastor of the church, my friend Eric VanBuskirk, who had been diagnosed with a very nasty blood cancer. He was undergoing treatment.

I felt strongly prompted by the Lord to call and say I would come as soon as possible to be with him and to pray for him. We talked through all the technical and medical details, and then the person started listing all of the things on the church calendar plus the Easter season and suggested that I come a couple of weeks after that. I responded, "Well, OK, if that's what you think. Love you and we'll be prayin' for you. Be in touch. Bye." I thought, *That's a couple of months away. I thought I was supposed to go immediately. Was I just over-reacting after the emotional shock of hearing that a vitally strong man of God was being mortally threatened?...*

Not ten minutes later, while I was still sorting through my thoughts, the phone rang again. "Mickey, God just spoke to me and said you are supposed to come right away!"

So I flew to Columbus, Ohio, because the VanBuskirk's home and church are 15 miles outside Chillocothe, Ohio. Church Triumphant is nestled beautifully in the middle of nowhere. It was a Saturday, unusually snowy, and I was quite surprised that Eric and his wife, Jeannette, were not in the big hospital in Columbus, but at home.

We fellowshipped. I listened to their medical journey as they joked about his "Mister Clean" image after his hair loss. As usual, they displayed their authentic faith and total trust in God. They had lived this way the entire time I had known them, and the church did as well. We agreed that I would preach the next morning and that I would lead the whole church in praying for him the next morning.

As I drove away from their home I was struck not so much by the seriousness of the cancer, but by their unwavering love and thankfulness to God, their Rock of strength. As I rounded the corner and passed in front of the church property, I felt the Holy Presence of God filling the car. Then I heard a Voice, and it said, "In the eyes of the world, people would say this is a small church. *This is one of my biggest churches*." I was numb. The thickness of the weight of glory remained in the car as I wove through the countryside back to my hotel room.

In the room, I turned on my laptop and started to work on what would be the beginnings of this book. After awhile, either blocked or bored, I turned on the TV, and then I fell asleep. I slept through the whole night, lights on, television blasting. When morning came, I woke up. *Wow, I've got to get to church now! I'm really a light sleeper. How did this happen?*

Scrambling to get ready, I went to my laptop, which was still on, having been on all night. Then I saw it—in boldface type over the top of my title page, the Holy Spirit had written a paragraph while I was sleeping. It started out, "I have lent you to these people for a specific purpose. Your life is not your own...." His word continued for about three or four more sentences, and I was not sure whether the content was meant to be personal or for the wider Body of Christ. It was about cleansing, holiness, forgiveness, the fruit of the Spirit, and being blameless before God.

What I *was* sure about was the awesome fear of the Lord. I have heard from Him many times and many ways with all kinds of manifestations, but never this way. As I read and re-read the paragraph, I was slammed with a stunning fear of the Lord.

The paragraph ended with the words, "...The Prophetic Made Personal."

I had to pack up my computer, and when I went to turn it off, the paragraph was gone. For a minute, I panicked. I wondered, *Did I mistakenly click "No" when it said "Do you want to save the changes you made to this document"?* Then I heard the voice of God again, "Do you want to save the changes I've made in your life?"

Direct hit. The prophetic *is* very personal. When He speaks to us, we learn wisdom and understanding, and yet we tremble at His word.

> *The fear of the Lord is the beginning of wisdom, and the knowledge of the Holy One is understanding* (Proverbs 9:10).

This is an eternal constant. May each one of us continue to come close enough to the Living God to hear His voice and to receive His cleansing touch, never forgetting that He Himself is the source of every good thing.

The Book of Acts describes the believers as being in a constant state of awe as many signs and wonders were taking place through the apostles. We certainly would benefit from not only singing songs about an awesome God, but experiencing Him as the only One who is ultimately awesome, even as we display a childlike expectancy of wondering what He will do next.

I did pray for Eric at the service that day, and I shared something (not everything because I didn't yet know if it was for everyone) about the paragraph the Holy Spirit had written on my computer the night before.

Eric was healed, and again he was cancer-free. Soon he had regained a full head of hair and he was back in the gym working out. He had never stopped preaching, teaching, and leading Church Triumphant.

Then about a year later, the cancer roared back. They fought heroically, but this kind was different. I never thought he would die from it, but on February 22, 2008, he went on to his reward.

The following July I was a guest speaker with my dear friend James Goll in Nashville. I was slotted to speak at the last main session. Back at the house, I was scurrying around getting ready, and the Lord told me to wear a red Nike golf shirt and black dress slacks. So I did.

At the church, I was no longer paying any more attention to my heavenly fashion advice, but rather trying to focus on my message. During worship, the Spirit said, "This is what Tiger Woods wears in the final round of every golf match. Tell My people I want you and all My people to finish well!" (This was during the time when Tiger was playing an amazing comeback victory with a torn ACL and a cracked tibia.)

That's the message: Finish well. No matter how lame the critics think the Church of the Lord is, He is going to straighten us out as we yield to Him. It's the theme of this book, and it's the theme of the Book. Making the prophetic personal is all about character—allowing His character to change ours.

I do not pretend to understand why Eric wasn't healed of cancer, nor do I like it, but what I do know is that he finished well. Church Triumphant is moving forward, and so are the rest of us. We do not question God's character, but rather celebrate it.

I heard about a young man who marveled at the perpetual, relentless enthusiasm of a stately elder prophet who just radiated. "How do you stay like that, sir?" asked the young prophet. "I never lost the wonder of it all," he replied with a twinkle in his eye.

When Jesus said, "It is finished," He provided all that is necessary for us to finish well. Not only do we have faith and wonder, we have His Spirit dwelling in our hearts, changing us into His likeness and speaking to us day by day, saying, *"'This is the way, walk in it,' whenever you turn to the right or to the left"* (Isa. 30:21).

Be encouraged; listen to His voice; go the distance!

A Sending Prayer

Father, You have created us for Your glory, and we know You have plans for our lives. We are grateful for the bodies, minds, and spirits with which You have created us, and we are especially grateful to You for activating our spirits by Your Spirit so that we have the ability to receive Your revelatory word.

Your living and active word is supernaturally sharp and powerful, and we ask You to open our spiritual eyes and ears to it. You are the Lord of wisdom and light and revelation. Adjust us so that we can receive from You everything that You want to give us.

For our part, Jesus, we desire You and Your word, which are one and the same. *"In the beginning was the Word, and the Word was with God, and the Word was God"* (John 1:1). Express Yourself to us and through us, Lord. Infiltrate our analytical minds and our earthbound hearts and bring to light anything that does not belong there. May we grow more like You even as You increase our receptivity to hear Your voice and to believe and obey what You tell us.

Release upon us a greater receptivity to Your voice. Come with power and set us free. Liberate us in Your love. Wash over us with Your cleansing stream and anoint us anew with the oil of Your Holy Spirit. Breathe new life into us so that we can perceive stirrings as deep calls to deep inside.

We see ourselves as vessels for carrying Your Spirit wherever we go. We are perceiving new things even now, and we are catching sight of new perspectives on subject matter we thought we knew well. So we are stepping into new freedom to become the prophetic people You destined us to be.

Holy Spirit, we are asking for grace to walk with You day by day, knowing that You will help us reach our full potential in You, bearing fruit for Your Kingdom. You are the living Word of God, dwelling within our hearts and revealing the truth to us with simple, vibrant eloquence. Our joy is in You, now and forever. Amen!

Additional copies of this book and other
book titles from DESTINY IMAGE are
available at your local bookstore.

Call toll-free: 1-800-722-6774.

Send a request for a catalog to:

Destiny Image® Publishers, Inc.

P.O. Box 310
Shippensburg, PA 17257-0310

*"Speaking to the Purposes of God for This
Generation and for the Generations to Come."*

**For a complete list of our titles,
visit us at www.destinyimage.com.**